Avoiding Nash Inflation

Bayesian and Robust Responses to Model Uncertainty

Robert Tetlow* and Peter von zur Muehlen
Federal Reserve Board
Washington, DC 20551

revised draft : April 2003

We examine learning, model misspecification, and robust policy responses to misspecification in a quasi-real-time environment. The laboratory for the analysis is the Sargent (1999) explanation for the origins of inflation in the 1970s and the subsequent disinflation. Three robust policy rules are derived that differ according to the extent that misspecification is taken as a parametric phenomenon. These responses to drifting estimated parameters and apparent misspecification are compared to the certainty-equivalent case studied by Sargent. We find gains from utilizing robust approaches to monetary policy design, but only when the approach to robustness is carefully tailored to the problem at hand. In the least parametric approach, the medicine of robust control turns out to be too potent for the disease of misspecification. In the most parametric approach, the response to misspecification is too weak and too misdirected to be of help. But when the robust approach to policy is narrowly directed in the correct location, it can avoid Nash inflation and improve social welfare. It follows that agnosticism regarding the sources of misspecification has its pitfalls. We also find that Sargent's story for the rise of inflation of the 1970s and its subsequent decline in the 1980s is robust to most ways of relaxing a strong assumption in the original work.

Keywords: uncertainty, Knightian uncertainty, robust control, learning, monetary policy.

JEL codes: C6, C8.

* Corresponding author. Robert.J.Tetlow@frb.gov, telephone: (202) 452-2437, facsimile: (202) 452-5297.
The authors thank Jagjit Chada, Tim Cogley, George Evans, Sean Holly, Seppo Honkapohja, Ken Kasa, Ben McCallum, Joe Pearlman, Mark Salmon and Tom Sargent for useful suggestions and encouragement. We also thank participants of "Workshop on Robustness", April 2003 at the Federal Reserve Bank of Cleveland, a 2003 AEA session in Washington, D.C., the conference on "Policy Rules: the next steps" at University of Cambridge, U.K., September 2002, and a Society for Computational Economics conference. All remaining errors are ours. The views expressed herein are those of the authors alone and are not necessarily shared by the Board of Governors or its staff.

1. Introduction:

> *In practice, it is the joining of ideas and data that drives policy in the face of uncertainty. We seek to array the probabilities of future policy outcomes, attempt to gauge the costs of being wrong in our decisions, and endeavor to choose the policy paths that appear to offer greater benefits and fewer risks...In practice, we continuously monitor [the] data to test the capability of any specific model. ...When we experience outcomes that do not square with what our models have projected, we form new hypotheses and reconstruct the models to more closely conform with our observations.*
>
> -- Alan Greenspan (2000), pp. 162-3.

It has long been recognized that the design of monetary policy is beset by uncertainties. As the words of the Chairman of the Federal Reserve indicate, there are two ingredients to the successful management of those uncertainties. The first, as epitomized by the second part of the quotation, has to do with adaptation of the central bank's model in response to the flow of data; that is, learning on the part of the central bank. The second, alluded to in the first part of the quotation, relates to policy design in the face of this evolving view on the economy and ever-present uncertainty that underlies this evolution. Both ingredients are critical.

This paper considers the design of monetary policy under uncertainty. Specifically, we use a simple model to jointly consider three things: learning by the monetary authority; model misspecification; and robust policies to counter the misspecification problems. To the best of our knowledge, this is the first paper to simultaneously consider these crucial elements of real-world policy design.

Our laboratory for this study is a very simple model studied in Sargent's (1999) monograph *The Conquest of American Inflation*, and then by Cho *et al.* (2002), Williams (2003) and Gerali and Lippi (2001). We re-examine Sargent's explanation for the inflation of the 1970s in the United States and the subsequent disinflation. According to Sargent, the rise of inflation in the 1970s and the subsequent fall in the early 1980s owes to bad inferences from the data. Central banks in general, and the Fed in particular, induced cycles in inflation because they were using the wrong model. And they used the wrong model because they incorrectly inferred structural parameters from reduced-form estimates.[1] This bad inference theory of inflation dynamics predicts that

---

1. An alternative theory is the so-called "bad luck theory" that prevailed in the 1970s. This view says that some bad shocks raised the inflation rate and also made disinflation unattractive to policy makers. The view lingers today: former Fed Vice-Chair Alan Blinder describes a variant of this view in his 1987 book. See De Long (1997) for a discourse on this subject and related themes.

the conquest of inflation in the United States is ephemeral; we are destined to relive the bad old days of the 1970s.[2] The Sargent model is ideal for our purposes for a number of reasons. First, it is simple enough to render some analytical results. Second, it has been studied before rendering us a foundation of knowledge upon which to build. Third, it provides a real-world but simple characterization of uncertainty and misspecification over time. Some papers evaluate the efficacy of various policies by exogenously specifying alternative true worlds, as in the rival-models methodology employed by Levin *et al.* (1999, 2001).[3] Others treat the misspecification as an abstract phenomenon as is typically done in robust control literature.[4] In this paper, we fully characterize the misspecification and its evolution as a part of the model.

The basic result is constructed in two steps. First, a hypothetical policymaker estimates a model of the economy using the latest available data, updating parameter estimates quarter-by-quarter. To do the estimation, the policymaker is assumed to use a constant-gain algorithm, described below, that allows for time variation in model coefficients. In employing constant-gain learning, the policy maker is embracing the second part of the Greenspan credo, noted at the outset, to adapt his or her view in response to surprises. Second, the estimated parameters are taken as given and the optimal policy is designed and carried out. Repeating these steps, over and over, results in episodic inflations—reaching what is called the Nash equilibrium—followed by "escapes" to lower inflation—the Ramsey equilibrium. This arises because at the low-inflation Ramsey equilibrium, the reduced-form estimates of the Lucas supply curve show favorable trade-offs for unemployment relative to inflation. Based on this inference, the authority engenders inflation surprises. But the surprises bring about an increase in inflation—and more generally a change in the time-series pattern of inflation—so that the favorable trade-off eventually disappears, and the Nash equilibrium obtains once again.[5] Eventually, a sequence of shocks arise that convince

---

2. See also DeLong (1997), Taylor (1997, 1998) and Cho, Williams and Sargent (2002) for arguments along these lines.
3. In the rival models framework, two or more models are considered simultaneously, one is taken to be the correct model, but no one knows which one. A policy is chosen that performs well in all of the candidate models, using any of a number of criteria.
4. See, *e.g.*, Hansen and Sargent (1995, 2003), Giannoni (2001, 2002), Tetlow and von zur Muehlen (2001b), Cho *et al.* (2002) and Kasa (2002), among others.
5. The classic references are Kydland and Prescott (1977) and Barro and Gordon (1983). Ireland (1999) provides a modern restatement and empirical assessment of the Barro-Gordon model. Along the same lines, Christiano and Gust (2000) argue that expectations of high inflation will be ratified by subsequent policy actions creating an "expectations trap". Their story differs from the present paper on the reasons why the Fed creates inflation: an expectations trap in their case and attempts to exploit a Phillips curve trade off in ours.

1. Introduction:

the policy maker that a new economy has arisen; then, based on this erroneous inference, the policymaker disinflates, and the process begins anew.

The main result—episodic Nash inflations followed by disinflations to the Ramsey solution—is built up from two key assumptions in the set-up: first, the assumption of the constant-gain estimation which acknowledges that from the authority's perspective, the economy is subject to drift in its structural parameters; and second, the assumption that notwithstanding this acknowledgment, the policymaker takes the estimated parameters at each date as the truth, and bases policy decisions on these values. Observing that the latter assumption is at odds with the former, one (narrow) way to look at the contribution of in this paper is that we relax the second assumption that the authority takes estimated parameters as given. Instead, while we retain the use of the constant-gain algorithm—or, equivalently, discounted recursive least squares—to update parameter estimates, we assume that the policymaker takes seriously the uncertainty in the estimates of these parameters. In so doing, we take on the first part of the Greenspan quotation noted above—to take seriously the prospects of unfavorable outcomes and protect against them—in a way that previous works in this strand of the literature have not.

We consider three different methods by which our policymaker might take uncertainty seriously. The approaches differ according to the extent to which model uncertainty is taken as a parametric phenomenon. The first of these methods, and the most parametric, is *Bayesian uncertainty*. Under the Bayesian approach to model uncertainty model parameters are assumed to have known distributions, the means and variances of which vary over time, and these variances are used to design policy.[6] The seminal references in this literature include Brainard (1967), Chow (1970) and Craine (1977). The second is *structured Knightian uncertainty* where the uncertainty is structured in the sense that it is located in one or more specific parameters of the model, but where the true values of these parameters are known only to be bounded between minimum and maximum conceivable values. Because the source of the misspecification is specified, but the nature is not, structured Knightian uncertainty is less parametric than the Bayesian approach. Among the expositors of this approach to model uncertainty are von zur Muehlen (1982), Giannoni (2001, 2002) and Svensson (2000).[7] The third method is *unstructured Knightian uncertainty*

---

6. Consistent with the rest of the literature in this area, the sense in which we describe our policy as "Bayesian" is restricted. The literature takes Bayesian to mean that the authority uses statistical criteria to determine the extent to which estimated coefficients may be mismeasured and uses those criteria to adjust policy. Not considered are Bayesian decision theoretic approaches, nor is "experimentation" to find the correct specification as in Wieland (2003) for example.

1. Introduction:

in which the model is assumed to be misspecified in some unstructured way leading to the formulation of a game played by the central banker against a "malevolent nature". This is the least parametric approach. References in this strand of the literature include Caravani (1995), Hansen and Sargent (1995, 2002), Onatski and Stock (2002), Cho et al. (2002) and Tetlow and von zur Muehlen (2001b).[8] We compare these potential solutions of the induction problem to the linear-quadratic Gaussian control (or certainty equivalent) solution promulgated by the Tinbergen-Theil tradition.

In considering policy responses to unstructured Knightian uncertainty, this part of the paper takes one part of Sargent's work and combines it with another. In so doing we are asking if Sargent's proposed solution to model misspecification alleviates Sargent's induction problem, itself a manifestation of model misspecification.[9]

We find that for plausible degrees of uncertainty, the Bayesian approach to uncertainty does not materially differ from the performance of a policy of ignoring uncertainty altogether. This result is of more than academic interest. The conduct of monetary policy under uncertainty has become a subject of active interest, both in the academic literature, and perhaps more importantly within central banks. Besides the Fed, the European Central Bank, the Bank of England, the Bank of Canada, Sveriges Riksbank (Sweden), the Reserve Bank of Australia, and the Reserve Bank of New Zealand have all released working papers assessing the Bayesian approach to model uncertainty.[10] At the risk of overgeneralizing the findings, these papers generally concur with

---

7. There is also another, different notion of structured model uncertainty in the sense of Knight. It differs from the method used here in that the authority is assumed to choose a policy rule that maximizes the set of models for which the economy is stable. See Onatski and Stock (2002) and Tetlow and von zur Muehlen (2001b).

8. Each of the senses in which our policymaker takes uncertainty seriously is based on the authority's ignorance of a structurally time-invariant model. Uncertainty can also be considered from "the other side" by considering the private sector's ignorance of the policy rule. Tetlow and von zur Muehlen (2001a) look at how the private sector's need to learn Taylor-type rules might affect the choice of the rule. Closer to the spirit of this paper, Bullard and Cho (2001) use the canonical New Keynesian macromodel to show that some Taylor-type rules that would be well-behaved in a world of full information allow liquidity traps to arise when private agents' expectations are based on a misspecified model.

9. That is, we take Hansen and Sargent's (1995) tools to Sargent's (1999) problem. In point of fact, however, Sargent (1999, p. 7) ascribes the particular induction problem studied here to Edmund Phelps.

10. A sampling of central bank papers on Bayesian uncertainty, in various forms, and its implications for monetary policy include Hall et al. (1999), Martin (1999) at the Bank of England, Schellenkens (1999) and Smets (2000) at the ECB, Shuetrim and Thompson (2000) at the Reserve Bank of Australia, Drew and Hunt (1999) at the Reserve Bank of New Zealand, Söderström (2000) at Sveriges Riksbank, and Srour (1999) at the Bank of Canada. Papers out of the Federal Reserve System in the United States have been legion, including Sack (2000), Rudebusch (2001), Orphanides et al. (2000) and Tetlow (2003).

1. Introduction:

former Fed Vice-Chairman Alan Blinder's (1998) assessment that central banks should "compute the direction and magnitude of [the] optimal policy move...then do less."[11]

While the Bayesian approach to uncertainty furnishes few benefits, we find that the Knightian approach to model uncertainty can do even worse, depending in part on the technique employed and the degree of uncertainty aversion. A policymaker applying the tools of unstructured Knightian uncertainty exacerbates the cycles of Nash inflation followed by escapes that the certainty-equivalent policy maker naively induces. For structured Knightian uncertainty, however, some parameterizations allow an improvement in performance relative to the certainty equivalent policy. Taken together, these results suggest that to be assured of an improvement in policy performance the policy maker needs to have some idea of the origins of his or her specification problem. Taking the error as a mere matter of sampling error is no help, but treating the error as utterly mysterious is also unhelpful. An approach that is focussed with regard to the sources of misspecification, but non-parametric on its nature, fares best.

Several papers, most notably Sargent and Williams (2003), examine the implications of different learning mechanisms and prior beliefs for the mean dynamics of inflation and the pattern of escapes either in this model or models much like it. Among the contributions of this paper is that it holds the learning aspect of the issue constant and addresses robust responses to the time variation in parameters. It is the first paper of which we are aware that considers the control of a misspecified model while putting up the plausible candidate methods for dealing with misspecification in a horse race. It is also the first paper to consider robust control together with aspects of learning and does so in a quasi-real-time environment. Finally, it relaxes a key assumption in the original Sargent (1999) monograph. The rest of the paper proceeds as follows. Immediately following this Introduction, we introduce the very simple model used in Sargent (1999) and review the methodology used there and here, to model escape dynamics from Nash equilibria. Section 3 provides a primer on Bayesian and robust control and applies it to this very simple example and presents our results. A fourth section sums up and concludes.

---

11. The quotation, from page 11 of Blinder (1998) is actually the former Fed Vice-Chairman's characterization of the lesson of Brainard, although he writes approvingly of it. Blinder's own methodology was to "use a wide variety of models and don't ever trust any one of them too much...[and to] simulate a policy on as many models as possible, throw out the outlier(s), and average the rest" (p. 12). In endnote 11 he notes that the optimal information-weighting procedure would require the use of a variance-covariance matrix. This is an example of the Bayesian approach to model uncertainty. As discussed below, robust control methods accept the first part of Blinder quotation—the part before the ellipses—but reject the second.

1. Introduction:

2. Methodology

In his 1999 monograph *The Conquest of American Inflation*, Thomas Sargent showed how the induction problem a policymaker faces can result in recurring bouts of inflation outbreaks, followed by disinflations. The induction problem is the situation the policymaker faces when he or she (wrongly) infers structural parameters from reduced-form estimates. Sargent's application, and the subsequent work by Cho *et al.* (2002), Williams (2003) and Gerali and Lippi (2001) is based on the Phillips curve trade-off and follows in the line of research that begins with Lucas (1972) and Sargent (1971), culminating in Lucas's critique (1976).

In Sargent (1999), the policymaker commits two related errors. First, while the policymaker allows for the possibility that the coefficients of the Phillips curve (or the Lucas supply curve) may evolve over time, no allowance is made for such time variation to influence the way policy is formulated. If this were the only error, however, the solution might simply be a matter of using constant-term adjustments, or time-varying coefficients models to correct the problem. The second problem—the one emphasized in Lucas (1976)—is that the policymaker does not understand his or her own role, as a part of the data generating process, in determining the evolution of the reduced-form parameters. In this paper, we relax the first of these assumptions. In this section, we lay out the simplest of the models that Sargent (1999) studies, the nature of the induction problem, and the updating procedure that the policymaker is assumed to use to gather information and make inferences.

2.1 the true model:

Sargent (1999) studies several models. Here we restrict our attention to the simplest—the static version of the classical Phillips curve—since doing so allows us to generate some results analytically. It is also the model that is closest in spirit to the pioneering work in Lucas (1972). Lastly, it has the advantage of keeping the notation simple; it allows us to eschew the use of time subscripts except where time variation in beliefs makes it necessary. The models consists of just two equations, a Lucas supply curve, and a crude policy reaction function:

$$U = U^* - \theta(\pi - E\pi) + \upsilon_1 \tag{1}$$

$$E\pi = \hat{\pi} + \upsilon_2 \tag{2}$$

where U and π are the unemployment and inflation rates, respectively; $E\pi$ is the mathematical expectation of inflation, conditional on information available at the end of period *t-1*, and $\hat{\pi}$ is the target rate of inflation set by the central bank. Rational expectations mean that: $E\pi = \pi$. In this simple model, $\hat{\pi}$ is taken as a control variable, and so equation (2) can be interpreted as a policy rule with a control error.

2.2 policy objectives:

Following Sargent (1999), the periodic loss function to be minimized is assumed to be quadratic in unemployment and inflation with the parameter λ measuring the disutility of unemployment relative to inflation:

$$L = \frac{1}{2}E[\lambda U^2 + \pi^2] \qquad (3)$$

This loss function should be thought of as the *ex post* loss that the authority uses to compute the performance of a given strategy. In some circumstances, the authority will choose policies *ex ante* based on criteria that include uncertainty aversion, as discussed below. After the fact, however, performance will be measured by equation (3).

2.3 Equilibrium concepts:

By substituting equation (1) into equation (3), we can solve for the central bank's payoff function:

$$r(\pi, E\pi) = \frac{1}{2}[\lambda(U^* - \theta(\pi - E\pi))^2 + \pi^2] \qquad (4)$$

Minimization of (4) by the choice of π yields the best-response function:

$$\hat{\pi} = \frac{\lambda\theta}{1 + \lambda\theta^2}U^* + \frac{\lambda\theta^2}{1 + \lambda\theta^2}E\pi \equiv B(E\pi) \qquad (5)$$

A *rational-expectations equilibrium* (REE) is a set of arguments, $U, \pi, E\pi$ that satisfies the structural model given by equation (1), and the rational expectations restriction that subjective and objective expectations coincide: $E\pi = \pi$. Note that the rational-expectations restriction can also be thought of as the best-response function of the collective of atomistic private agents. A *Nash equilibrium* (NE) is a pair of arguments, $\pi, E\pi$ that lies on the best-response function of both the central bank and private agents. That is, it satisfies $\hat{\pi} = B(E\pi)$ and $E\pi = \hat{\pi}$. The presence of $E\pi$ as an argument to the NE reflects the fact that in computing the NE, the policymaker takes private-sector inflation expectations as given. Given equation (5), the NE for this economy is:

$$\hat{\pi}^n = \lambda\theta U^* \tag{6}$$

Equation (6) shows that inflation varies positively with the distaste of unemployment in the authority's loss function, the slope of the Lucas supply curve, and the natural rate of unemployment.

The *Ramsey equilibrium* (RE) differs from the Nash equilibrium in that the central bank is assumed to have the power to choose expected inflation, rather than taking it as given. This is equivalent to saying the central bank has a commitment technology that allows it to deliver (up to a random error), a given inflation rate for all time that is then ratified by agents' expectations.[12] Thus, the RE is defined by $r(\pi, \pi)$ and is the solution to the problem:

$$\hat{\pi} = \underset{\langle\pi\rangle}{\operatorname{argmin}} \, r(\pi, \pi) = \underset{\langle\pi\rangle}{\operatorname{argmin}} \, \frac{1}{2}[\lambda(U^* - \theta(\pi - E\pi))^2 + \pi^2] \tag{7}$$

subject to $E\pi = \pi = \hat{\pi}$. Substituting this condition into equation (7) and differentiating renders:

$$\hat{\pi}^r = 0 \tag{8}$$

So in the presence of a commitment technology that would make the Ramsey equilibrium feasible, the policymaker would set the inflation rate to zero. By comparison, adopting as we do the same calibration as Sargent (1999, chapter 7), $\{U^*, \lambda, \theta\} = \{5, 1, 1\}$, the Nash equilibrium implies the setting of a positive inflation rate: $\hat{\pi}^n = 5$.

3. Controlling an Uncertain Economy

Section 2 discussed the true data generating process for the economy and reviewed the equilibrium concepts that define the full-information equilibria. In this section, we introduce our departure from the full-information environment. We begin by specifying the perceived model of the economy; that is, the econometric equation estimated by the monetary authority in the Tinbergen-Theil tradition. Then we discuss the method by which the authority updates his or her model of the economy over time. Finally, we address our four models of control, beginning with the linear-quadratic Gaussian (LQG), or certainty equivalent case. From there, we study the Bayesian prescription for parameter uncertainty: adjusting the LQG response for uncertainty as captured by the standard error of parameter estimates. Then we study robust policy from the perspective of

---

12. One way to think of the Ramsey equilibrium as compared to the Nash equilibrium is from the perspective of game theory. The RE is the Stackelberg game counterpart to the Nash game.

structured and unstructured model uncertainty. In each subsection, we characterize the authority's decision rule and compute the paths for inflation and the rule parameters.

3.1 the perceived model:

Let the central bank's perceived model be:

$$U = \gamma_0 + \gamma_1 \pi + \varepsilon + \omega \tag{9}$$

where ε is a random error, taken to be independently and identically distributed, and ω is a distortion representing possible specification errors. When designing robust policy, ω is taken as the instrument of a hostile opponent (nature) in a Stackelberg game, as we shall outline a bit later. In the special case where $\omega = 0$, and the estimated parameters are taken as if they were known, policy is certainty equivalent. To this point, the presence of ω is the only discrepancy from the environment that Sargent describes. The policymaker chooses a set of feedback coefficients, F, of the perceived model's parameters to guide policy:

$$\hat{\pi} = F(\gamma_0, \gamma_1)Z \tag{10}$$

where, in general, $Z = (1, U)'$. Simply put, our policymaker runs a regression, of a particular type to be discussed below, to extract regression coefficients, γ_i, $i = 0, 1$, and then uses these estimates to formulate policy. If the policymaker knows the true parameters of the model, the certainty-equivalent (linear-quadratic Gaussian, or LQG) policy corresponds with the (discretionary) Nash equilibrium. The question is whether the authority's ignorance of his or her own role in generating misspecifications is sufficient for any or all of the approaches for responding to uncertainty to dominate the LQG criteria. Sargent (1999) assesses the LQG criteria for controlling the economy, effectively ignoring the model uncertainty that using the constant-gain algorithm for updating coefficient estimates explicitly admits. We relax this restriction. The ways in which we do this, and the results we obtain, are studied in the next section.

3.2 discounted recursive least squares:

As in Sargent (1999), we assume that the policymaker updates estimates of the economy on a period-by-period basis. If this were done using least squares, the gain from adding periods of observations would be $1/t$, which converges on zero as $t \to \infty$. This is sensible provided one accepts that the true economy is time invariant. Under such circumstances, the first observation in a time series is just as valuable for discerning the true parameters as the most-recent observation. If, however, the policymaker wishes to entertain the possibility that the true model parameters shift over time, he or she may wish to weight recent observations more heavily than distant ones. This can be done by utilizing discounted recursive least squares, otherwise known as constant-gain learning:

$$\gamma_{t+1} = \gamma_t + g P_t^{-1} X_t (U_t - \gamma_t X_t) \tag{11}$$

$$P_{t+1} = P_t + g(X_t X_t' - P_t) \tag{12}$$

where $\gamma_t = [\gamma_{0t}\ \gamma_{1t}]'$, $X_t = [1\ \pi_t]$ and $g = 1 - \rho$ with ρ being a 'forgetting factor' measuring the rate at which old information is discounted. Note that we now show time subscripts reflecting the evolution, as perceived by the policymaker, of coefficients over time. Equations (11) and (12) differ from recursive least squares only in that the gain associated with each new observation is fixed at a constant, g, instead of a variable that is strictly decreasing in time. In equation (11), the vector γ_t is the t-dated slice of the 2-by-t period vector time series of estimated model parameters; P_t is the "precision matrix" as of date t (and a part of a 2-by-2-by-T vector time series); and the term in parentheses is the observation error in the regression that the policymaker conducts. So equation (11) says the change in the estimated parameters is a weighted function of the observation error. In equation (12), the precision matrix is shown to evolve according to a constant proportion, g, of the discrepancy between the variance-covariance matrix of observed regression variables, XX', and the inherited precision. The constant gain has a natural Bayesian interpretation in that g can be thought of as the arrival rate of unobservable regime shifts.

In addition, for two of the cases we study below, we condition policy responses on estimates of the standard error of parameter estimates. To facilitate this calculation in the (pseudo) real-time environment we work with, we model the mean squared error, M, and the 2-by-2 matrix of standard errors, σ, in a fashion analogous to equations (11) and (12) above:

$$M_{t+1} = M_t + g[(U_t - \gamma_t X_t)^2 - M_t] \tag{13}$$

$$\sigma_{t+1} = M_{t+1}/P_{t+1} \tag{14}$$

Equations (11) and (12) constitute a learning rule, but certainly not the only one that we could have specified. Our choice of this particular one reflects our focus in this paper on the issue

3. Controlling an Uncertain Economy

of control of the economy, taking as given a simple model of learning. It also reflects its prior use by Sargent. A different approach would have been to address whether and how a misinformed central banker might come to learn the true structure of the economy. However, since a part of what we focus on presumes that the authority does not believe the true model is learnable, a detailed investigation of learning models would be a sizable digression for this paper.

With the true economy specified by equations (1) and (2), and the most general specification of the estimated economy being equation (9), the system can be set in motion, drawing shocks, $\upsilon = \begin{bmatrix} \upsilon_{1t} & \upsilon_{2t} \end{bmatrix}$, generating observed variables, $X = \begin{bmatrix} U_t & \pi_t \end{bmatrix}$, from which regression coefficients $\gamma = \begin{bmatrix} \gamma_{0t} & \gamma_{1t} \end{bmatrix}$ are derived. Then, based on the estimated coefficients, the authority chooses a response function.

3.3 the optimal certainty-equivalent rule

With LQG optimization, we can write the Lagrangian for the authority's problem as:[13]

$$\min_{\langle \pi \rangle} \frac{1}{2}[\lambda U^2 + \pi^2] + \phi[U - \gamma_0 - \gamma_1 \pi] \tag{15}$$

where we note that the policymaker has taken ω_t, in equation (9), to be zero. The problem yields the following first-order conditions:

$$\pi - \gamma_1 \phi = 0 \tag{16}$$

$$\lambda U + \phi = 0 \tag{17}$$

from which we can write the target rate of inflation as:

$$\hat{\pi}^{ce} = -\lambda \gamma_1 U = -\lambda \gamma_0 \gamma_1 / (1 + \lambda \gamma_1^2) \tag{18}$$

where the second equality comes from substituting in equation (9) with $E\varepsilon = 0$. Note that the first equality is the same as for the Nash equilibrium--when $\gamma_1 = -\theta$. In the true economy, agents take the authority's inflation target as given and, basing inflation expectations on that target, react accordingly. Substituting $\hat{\pi}^{ce}$ into equation (1), the implied paths of unemployment and inflation are:

$$\pi_t = -\lambda \gamma_{0t} \gamma_{1t} / (1 + \lambda \gamma_{1t}^2) + \upsilon_{2t} \tag{19}$$

---

13. Once again, we elect to suppress the time subscripts and the evolution of beliefs in recognition that the policymaker takes the evolution of the estimated parameters as a random process.

$$U_t = U_t^* - \theta\upsilon_{2t} + \upsilon_{1t} \qquad (20)$$

With, $\sigma_{\upsilon 1} = \sigma_{\upsilon 2} = 0.3$, also taken from Sargent (1999), equations (19) and (20) become the (true) data-generating process from which the policymaker re-estimates parameters $\gamma = \begin{bmatrix} \gamma_{0t} & \gamma_{1t} \end{bmatrix}$ through time.

A stochastic simulation of the system under constant-gain learning with $\rho = 0.9725$ is shown in Figure 1. As Sargent (1999), Cho *et al.* (2002), Kasa (2003), and Williams (2003) have shown, when the policymaker uses a constant-gain algorithm, like the discounted recursive least squares algorithm used here, the model generates escape dynamics wherein the economy will tend towards the Nash equilibrium, so long as the perceived trade-off between inflation and unemployment is regarded as favorable; that is, when $-E\theta = \gamma_1 \approx \gamma_1^n = -1$. Under such conditions, the policymaker, taking γ_{1t} as predetermined, can produce large decreases in unemployment for a monetary surprise of a given size. The ultimate result, however, is to raise the inherited inflation rate each period until it is high enough that the marginal benefits of inflation surprises are no longer larger than the costs. This is the Nash equilibrium. As is well known, under least-squares learning, the Nash equilibrium is self-fulfilling, meaning that there is no tendency for the monetary authority to doubt its beliefs of the structure of the economy in the presence of stochastic shocks. Under constant-gain learning, however, the Nash equilibrium is not sustainable.

Once the Nash equilibrium is obtained, a sequence of shocks eventually arises that makes it worthwhile for the authority to disinflate—to "escape" from the Nash equilibrium. During the course of an escape, the perceived slope falls, in absolute terms, from its Nash equilibrium level of minus one, to nearly zero. Given this new-found belief, the optimal policy is to set inflation near zero: This is the Ramsey equilibrium. In the neighborhood of the Ramsey equilibrium—that is, when $\gamma_1 = \gamma_1^r \approx 0$—the authority believes in a (distorted) version of the natural rate hypothesis, accepts that there is no trade-off between inflation and unemployment, and therefore does not try to produce inflation surprises. However once the Phillips curve becomes vertical, the random disturbances lead the authority to back to the Nash equilibrium.

Figure 1
Inflation Performance and Perceived Supply Curve Parameters
Linear-quadratic gaussian (LQG), or certainty equivalent, policy

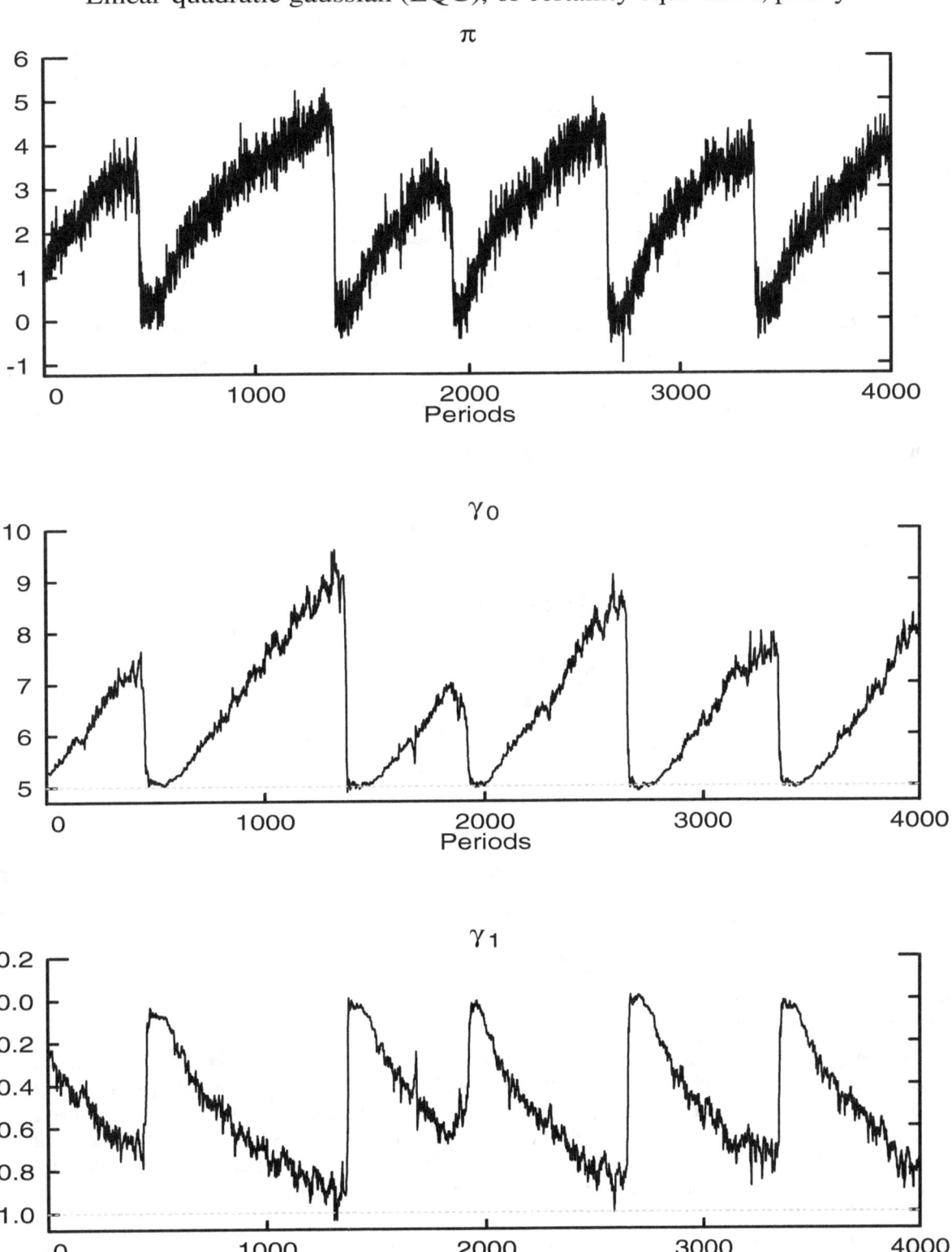

3. Controlling an Uncertain Economy

In fact, the economy rarely gets close to its Nash equilibrium before a chance sequence of shocks combines with the perceived steepness of the supply curve to induce a disinflationary episode. The precise timing of escapes from Nash inflation depends on the sequence of shocks. Cho *et al.* (2002) and Williams (2003) discuss the necessary conditions in some detail. Nonetheless, the pattern described in the text is clear: recurring episodes of rising inflation, reaching near the Nash equilibrium, followed by discrete disinflations; and then the process begins anew.

3.4 the optimal Bayesian rule

As argued above, discounted learning is based on the notion that parameters vary over time. Yet the LQG policymaker ignores this idea when setting the policy response. The Sargent characterization of policymaking seems contradictory in this sense. One possible response to the parameter variation shown in Figure 1 is to take it as a purely statistical phenomenon, much like Blinder (1998), following Brainard (1967), has advocated.[14] In present circumstances, this amounts to respecifying the loss function as follows:

$$\hat{\pi}^b = \mathop{\mathrm{argmin}}_{\langle \pi \rangle} E\frac{1}{2}[\lambda U^2 + \pi^2]$$

$$= \mathop{\mathrm{argmin}}_{\langle \pi \rangle} \left[E\frac{1}{2}\pi^2 + \lambda \frac{1}{2} E(\gamma_0 + \gamma_1 \pi)^2 \right] \quad (21)$$

$$= \mathop{\mathrm{argmin}}_{\langle \pi \rangle} \left[\frac{1}{2} \lambda E\gamma_0^2 + \frac{1}{2}(1 + \lambda E\gamma_1^2)\pi^2 + \lambda E\gamma_0\gamma_1\pi \right] \quad (22)$$

where we have assumed that the error terms, υ_1 and υ_2 are independent, and as before, $E\pi = \hat{\pi}$. Let σ represent the matrix of standard errors associated with the estimated γ_i, and $\psi \geq 1$ represent an uncertainty aversion parameter, of sorts. If $\psi = 1$, the authority lets its uncertainty aversion be represented simply by σ, and the response to parameter uncertainty is determined in the familiar way. Purely for demonstrative purposes however, we allow the authority to consider adopting a $\psi > 1$ which can be thought of as representing a distrust of the estimated model that exceeds that which would be determined by unquestioned econometric criteria alone; this distrust,

---

14. Cogley and Sargent (2001) in a thorough and interesting paper use Bayesian econometrics to address the drift in estimated coefficients over time that the Fed would observe and the consequent likelihood of "forgetting the natural rate hypothesis". Their paper differs in many ways from ours. One is that drifting parameters are assumed to follow a random walk in their paper whereas here they evolve according to the specification error and subsequent policy errors the policy maker commits. More generally, they do not consider robust policies in response to parameter drift. One way to think about how the Bayesian control case here differs from standard work is that the dynamics of misspecification here generate time variation in coefficients that violate the usual assumption in Bayesian analysis that coefficients follow a random walk. We are grateful to Tim Cogley for pointing this fact out to us.

however, manifests itself in the usual Bayesian way in that it is intimately connected to the precision of estimated parameters over time. With this in mind, the first-order condition for this problem can then be written as:

$$0 = (1 + \lambda E\gamma_1^2)\pi + \lambda E\gamma_0\gamma_1 = [1 + \lambda(\gamma_1^2 + \psi\sigma_{\gamma 1}^2)]\pi + \lambda(\gamma_0\gamma_1 + \psi\sigma_{\gamma 0\gamma 1}) \quad (23)$$

which implies that the policymaker's optimal inflation target is:

$$\hat{\pi}^b = \frac{-\lambda(\gamma_0\gamma_1 + \psi\sigma_{\gamma 0\gamma 1})}{1 + \lambda(\gamma_1^2 + \psi\sigma_{\gamma 1}^2)} \quad (24)$$

In equation (24), the inflation target for the Bayesian policymaker differs from the LQG policy in equation (18) only in the presence of ψ, and the terms in σ, which will vary over time. So the difference over time in the performance of the economy under the two policies (holding constant the sequence of shocks to which the economy is subjected) is in the matrix, σ, and the associated differences in the vector, γ. A value of $\psi > 1$ accentuates whatever effect that $\sigma > 0$ might have. The effect of $\sigma_{\gamma 1}$ is attenuating in its implications for policy: that is, relative to the LQG or certainty equivalent policy, it reduces the target inflation rate, all else equal. The effect of $\sigma_{\gamma 0\gamma 1}$ could be attenuating, or anti-attenuating. Moreover, it is also worth recalling that generally $\gamma^n \neq \gamma^b$. It follows that the Bayesian policy could call for policy that is more, or less, aggressive than the CE policy.

In fact, using the same parameters and the same sequence of random shocks as in Figure 1, and setting $\psi = 1$, the performance of the economy under the control of the Bayesian policymaker differs only marginally from that of the LQG policy, as shown in Figure 2a. The Bayesian policy supports Nash and Ramsey equilibria with about the same inflation rates as in the LQG case, although there is one fewer escape than in the LQG case. The facts are that despite the misspecification of the model, the time variation in the estimated parameters is insufficient to induce a substantial alteration the designated policy. In this model, the t-statistic associated with the intercept is high. However, equation (24) indicates that it is the precision of the slope coefficient that matters. In fact, the absolute t-statistic on γ_1 is generally low, particularly in the neighborhood of the Ramsey equilibrium. So the Bayesian response to this imprecision is not substantial despite the fact that the estimate of the key slope parameter is not a good one. Blinder's advocacy of the Brainard principle notwithstanding, a straight-forward application of the Bayesian approach to model uncertainty offers no solution to the problem studied here.

It is worth emphasizing that this result obtains despite the use of constant-gain learning. By shortening the effective horizon over which the standard errors are computed, shown in equations (12), (13) and (14), constant-gain learning has a tendency to blow up standard errors from what they would be under least-squares learning. Thus, even with $\psi = 1$, we are allowing some policymaker skepticism creep into his or her decision making, to little avail.

There are at least some hints of this result in the literature. It is primarily in papers that work with artificial examples, such as Brainard's original 1967 paper, and more recently Söderström (1999) that uncertainty in the Bayesian sense has appeared to matter. In papers that employ real-world examples such as the attempts by Sack (2000) and Rudebusch (2001) to explain the observed "timidity" of U.S. monetary policy, uncertainty has been insufficient as an explanation.[15]

Now suppose the authority behaved as if the estimated standard errors were much higher; in particular, suppose it set $\psi = 5$, which is arguably a substantial degree of uncertainty aversion. Figure 2b shows that when a Bayesian policymaker controls the economy in this way, the same general pattern emerges: Nash and Ramsey equilibria are about the same as in the LQG, but the escapes from the Nash equilibria are even less frequent than before. In fact, there is just one escape during the period shown in the figure. However, while the reduction in the number of escapes avoids some cycling in the economy, it does so at the cost of keeping inflation at the higher Nash rate of five percent for longer periods; as such, welfare is actually lower under the Bayesian response to model uncertainty than it is under LQG, as we shall discuss later on.

---

15. It has been suggested to us that a Bayesian policymaker that engages in optimal experimentation might turn in a better performance than what is suggested here. We do not undertake this line of enquiry here for four reasons. First, it takes us away from our main concern which is robust policy making and diverts it to the important but separate issue of learning. (Tetlow and von zur Muehlen (2003) take up certain issues involving the choice of learning mechanisms.) Second, considering experimentation by the Bayesian policymaker would eliminate the "fair fight" aspect of the current comparison by giving the Bayesian an advantage over the alternatives. Third, Beck and Wieland (2002) show in a model not very different from ours that it is not optimal for an authority to do experimentation. The reason is that in a world where the time-inconsistency problem is at work the cost of experimentation in an economy is higher than the benefit of a greater flow of information owing to the distortion. And fourth, we know by the nature of the misspecification problem here that it is not a deficiency of statistical information that underlines the problem.

Figure 2a
Response to Bayesian Parameter Risk
($\psi = 1$)

π

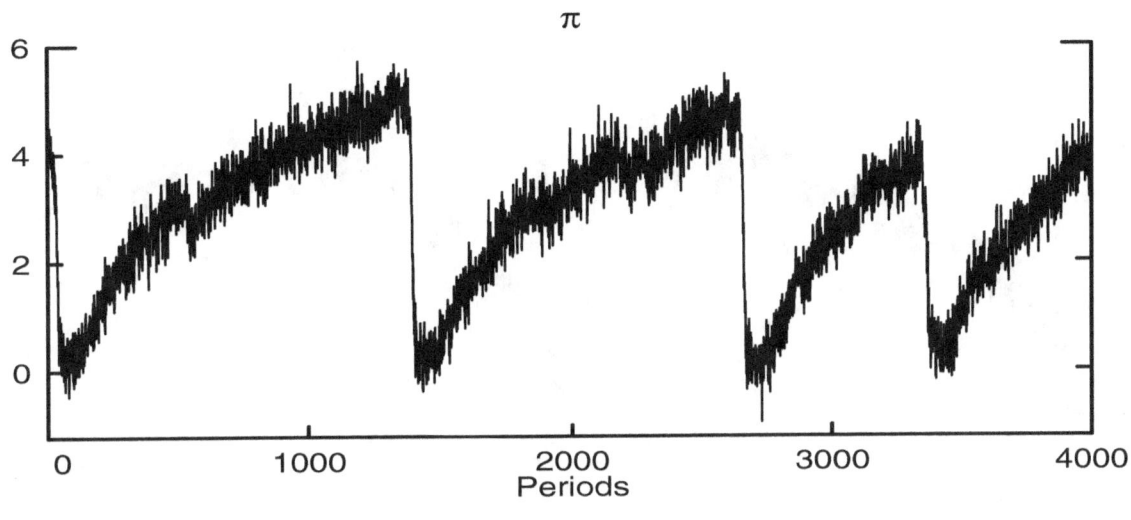

γ_0

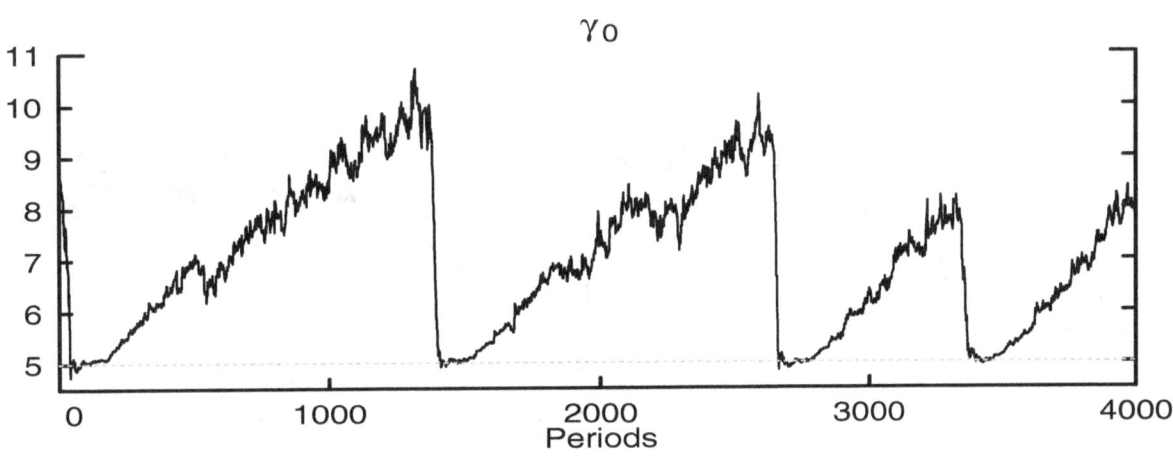

γ_1

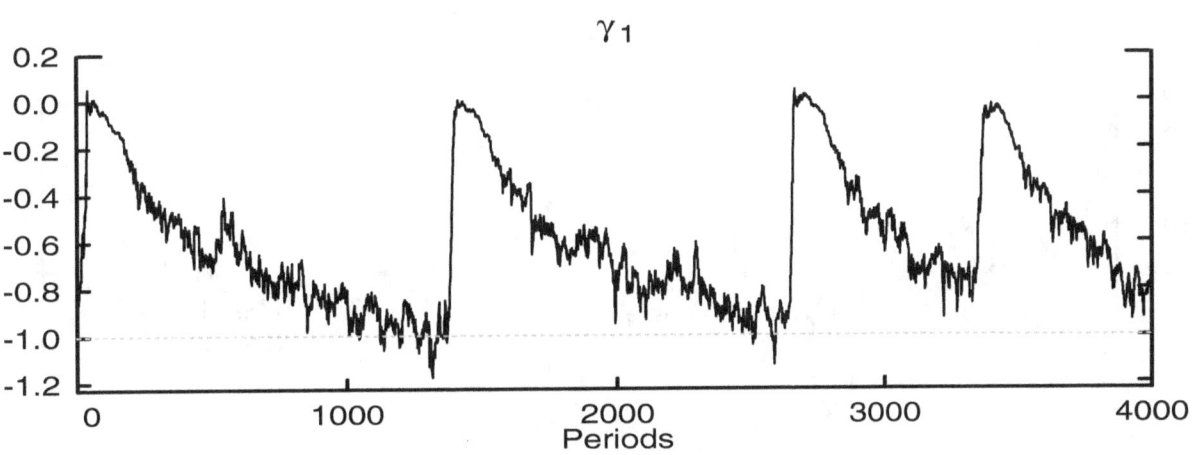

Figure 2b
Response to Bayesian Parameter Risk
(Robustness preference, $\psi = 5$)

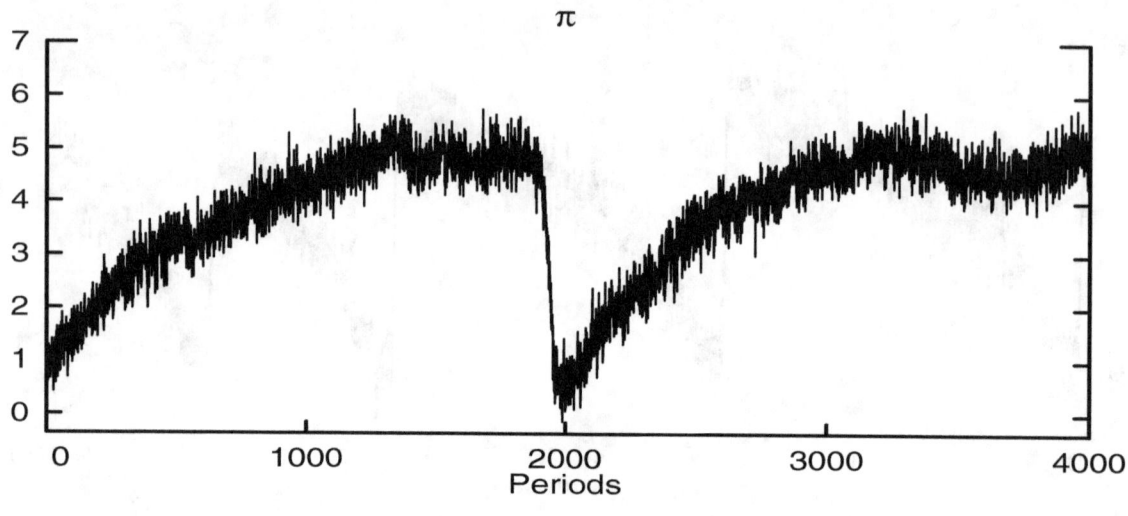

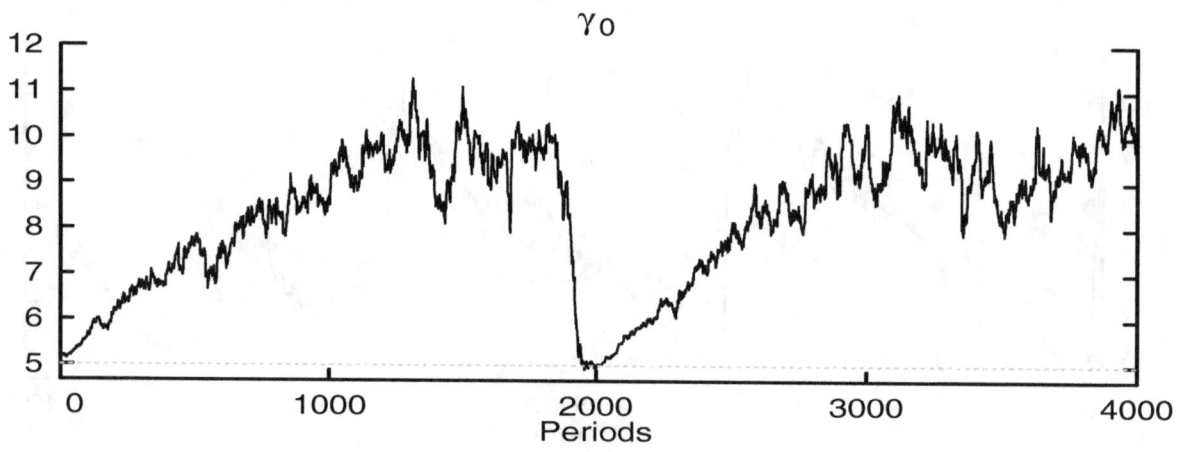

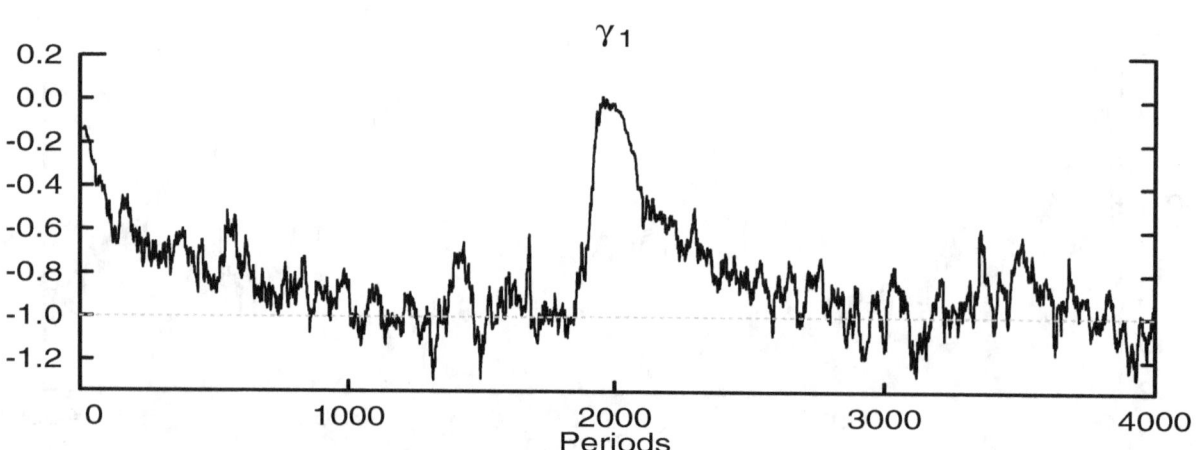

3. Controlling an Uncertain Economy

3.5 robust policy I: unstructured model uncertainty

In this subsection and the next one, we consider a policymaker that takes a more jaundiced view of the specification of the model. In particular, the authority is now assumed to behave as if the model were misspecified in an imprecise way. In the present subsection, we consider *unstructured model uncertainty*, where the authority is assumed to have a *reference model* that is approximately correct, but faces local Knightian uncertainty the model's specification, the location of which is unspecified. The difference from the Bayesian concept of parameter uncertainty discussed in the previous subsection is three fold: First, in this subsection, the authority is assumed not to have a prior on the location of the model's possible misspecification; it could be misspecified parameters, shock processes, or a missing non-linearity. Second, because the authority accepts that its problem stems from misspecification, as opposed to sampling error, no standard error is assigned to the uncertainty. The best the policymaker can do is to specify a neighborhood within which the uncertainty is assumed to lie. Third, having defined a set of models within which the true model is believed to exist, the policymaker is assumed to conduct policy to minimize the worst-case outcome within that set. That is, the authority solves a minimax problem. Sworder (1965) and Gilboa and Schmeidler (1989) show how Knightian uncertainty leads to a minimax specification for decision making. Utilizing a minimax criterion ensures that the authority has chosen a rule that will perform adequately for any model within the allowable set. An alternative but equivalent way of thinking about unstructured model uncertainty in relation to Bayesian parameter uncertainty is that the former is as non-parametric as is feasible while the latter is parametric.

It is important to recognize that the set of allowable models need not be large and need not include wildly improbable models. Provided that the range of models contained within the allowable set is "reasonable", there is nothing paranoid in the authority's response to model uncertainty.[16] This is not the only way in which one can specify model uncertainty in the sense of Knight. In the next subsection, we shall specify another, more structured notion of Knightian uncertainty, where the assumption that the location of model misspecification is unknown is dropped. That is, we will grant the authority knowledge of the location of the misspecification, but not enough about its nature to assign probabilities to model parameters.

---

16. In fact, von zur Muehlen (1982) shows that for a linear model, the minimax solution to structured Knightian uncertainty is the same response one would obtain for a uniform distribution of parameters. Under either assumption, the only relevant cases are the boundary values for the parameters.

Without a location for the uncertainty, all specification errors appear to our authority as a vector of residuals. As Hansen and Sargent (1995, 2002) have argued, this results quite naturally in the policymaker acting as though he or she were the leader in a two-player Stackelberg game played against a "malevolent nature". The idea is that the misspecification is of unknown origin, but it will show up as outsized and deleterious residuals just when the policymaker attempts to exploit the model, conditional on the estimated parameters, to achieve policy objectives. The authority is best able to avoid disappointment by acting as though nature gets to choose a sequence of shocks to *maximize* the policymaker's loss, within some bounds, after the policymaker has chosen a policy rule. It follows that the policymaker will choose the rule for which the maximum loss that can be inflicted by nature is at its minimum. Getting beyond the Stackelberg game metaphor, what this set-up does is ensure that the chosen rule is optimal for the complete class of models in the allowable set.

In terms of equation (9), robustness against unstructured model uncertainty is invoked by activating the expectations distortion variable—that is, the "residual," ω_t. The assumption that the reference model is taken only to be an approximation of the truth is captured by an added constraint, equation (25) below, on what would otherwise be the standard LQG problem of the minimization of equation (15):

$$\omega^2 \leq \eta^2 \qquad |\eta| < \infty \qquad (25)$$

A small value for η reflects an assumption on the part of the authority that the approximation of the reference model is a close one. We use Hansen and Sargent (2002) as a guide to specify the following multiplier game:

$$\max_{\pi} \sup_{\theta > 0} \inf_{\omega} -\frac{1}{2}(1 + \lambda\gamma_1^2)\pi^2 - \frac{1}{2}\lambda\omega^2 - \lambda\gamma_0\gamma_1\pi - \lambda\gamma_0\omega - \lambda\gamma_1\omega\pi - \frac{1}{2}\lambda\gamma_0^2 + \frac{1}{2}\mu(\omega^2 - \eta^2) \quad (26)$$

where μ is the Lagrange multiplier associated with the constraint imposed on optimization by nature's attempt to do damage to our policymaker's plans. In the game laid out in equation (26), the value of μ is, in some sense, a choice parameter, reflecting the extent to which the authority wishes to protect against uncertain damage.[17] Hansen and Sargent refer to μ as a preference for robustness. Nature's influence on welfare is more limited as $\mu \to \infty$; when $\mu = \infty$ the authority chooses not to protect against model uncertainty (or equivalently there is no *ex ante* model uncertainty). As μ falls, the authority's preference for robustness is increasing and consequently nature's influence on policy is rising. When μ reaches λ, policy is at its most uncertainty aversive; this is the H^∞ solution; see, e.g., Whittle (1990, pp. 207-13), Caravani (1995). Thus, the value μ in this problem of unstructured model uncertainty plays a role comparable to that of the extreme bounds in the structured model uncertainty problem of the previous subsection. There is also a connection between unstructured model uncertainty and the Bayesian approach to uncertainty covered in subsection 3.4. Adam (2002) shows that the H^∞ problem can be thought of as the selection of an objective function wherein the choice of the optimal Bayesian decision rule is invariant to any non-degenerative set of priors over the models in the allowable set. That is, the H^∞ rule is the optimal Bayesian rule in a world where priors are unknown and there are no well-defined priors over the priors.

Substituting for U using equation (9), the first-order conditions with respect to $\hat{\pi}$ and ω are:

$$-(1+\lambda\gamma_1^2)\pi - \lambda\gamma_1\omega - \lambda\gamma_0\gamma_1 = 0 \qquad (27)$$

$$-\lambda\gamma_1\pi + (\mu-\lambda)\omega - \lambda\gamma_0 = 0 \qquad (28)$$

Equation (28) clearly shows that the magnitude of μ matters in determining the outcome, and since μ determines ω, it matters for equation (27) as well.

Satisfaction of the second-order condition for equation (28) requires $\mu - \lambda \geq 0$. When $\mu = \lambda$, the loss function is affine with respect to ω, meaning there is no uncertainty aversion. Were μ permitted to be less than λ, this would be tantamount to assuming the policymaker is an uncertainty seeker, in which case nature would always choose $\omega = -\infty$ guaranteeing the maximum possible loss to the authority. Thus the minimum value for μ is λ—that is, the H^∞ solution—plus a small increment. When μ gets large, the solution approaches the LQG solution as we shall presently show.

Solving the first-order conditions for π and ω, and using the u superscript to note solution values for the unstructured model uncertainty problem, we have:

---

17. We say in the text that μ is a choice parameter "in some sense" because there is the delicate, almost existential issue of whether one can choose how much to hedge against model misspecification of a given magnitude, or whether that parameter is given by tastes. Formally, the "choice" of μ is directly determined by the magnitude of uncertainty, η. This is easy to see in the present example: Solve equation (28) for μ and set $|\omega| = |\eta|$, this being nature's best choice when $\mu > \lambda$. This gives $= \lambda(1+|\gamma_0+\gamma_1\pi|/\imath$. Looking at this, we can see that as $\eta \to 0, \imath \to \infty$ and when $\eta \to \infty, \imath \to \lambda$. This implies a direct relationship between η μ and in this sense, the two are inextricable.

3. Controlling an Uncertain Economy

$$\hat{\pi}^u = \frac{-\lambda\gamma_0\gamma_1}{1 + \lambda\gamma_1^2 - \lambda/\mu} \qquad (29)$$

$$\omega = \frac{\lambda\gamma_0}{\mu(1 + \lambda\gamma_1^2) - \lambda} \qquad (30)$$

Notice that as the penalty on nature's control, μ, rises towards infinity, ω approaches zero, and $\pi \to -\lambda\gamma_0\gamma_1/(1 + \lambda\gamma_1^2)$ which is the certainty equivalent solution. Conversely, as $\mu \to \underline{\mu} = \lambda$, ω approaches $\gamma_0/\lambda\gamma_1^2$ from below and $\pi \to -\gamma_0/\gamma_1$.[18]

When the policymaker has doubts about the veracity of the reference model, inflation will be higher than in the certainty equivalent case (holding constant γ):

$$\hat{\pi}^u - \hat{\pi}^{ce} = \frac{\lambda\gamma_0\gamma_1/\mu}{(1 + \lambda\gamma_1^2)(1 + \lambda\gamma_1^2 - \lambda/\mu)} > 0 \qquad \mu < \infty \qquad (31)$$

It is easy to show that Ramsey equilibrium remains at zero and equation (31) implies that the Nash inflation rate will be higher than its counterpart under the certainty equivalent policy, all else equal. If could assume that the $\gamma^u = \gamma^{ce}$, we would have no need to run the simulation; we would know *a priori* that unstructured robust policymaking produces more volatility and higher average rates of inflation than the certainty equivalent policy. However, feedback of policy to subsequent estimates of γ means that in general $\gamma^u \neq \gamma^{ce}$.

The preceding has shown how unstructured model uncertainty, and the policymaker's aversion to it, can be modeled as a two-player game, and equivalently as a multiplier problem with the weight on the multiplier representing the authority's aversion to uncertainty. With this in mind, in Figures 3a and 3b, we show the dynamic solutions for our model economy with two different settings for μ: $\mu = \lambda + 0.01$—which is close to the H^∞ solution, the most highly uncertainty-averse solution that is feasible—and $\mu = \lambda + 0.1$ which is somewhat uncertainty aversive.

Figure 3a exhibits extreme swings in inflation. The dependence of inflation on the value of μ, shown analytically in equation (29), is dramatically demonstrated by the heights reached at various periods in the upper panel of the figure. At the same time, escapes to lower inflation rates

---

18. Note that the self-confirming equilibrium--that is, the equilibrium at which the authority would not conclude that his or her working model of the economy is misspecified--is, for the unstructured robust controller: $= \lambda\theta(1 + \theta^2)U^*/[1 + \lambda\theta^2 - \lambda/$ which becomes the NE as $\mu \to \infty$. By contrast, as $\mu \to \lambda$ (from above) the solution converges on the H^∞ solution. With $U^* = 5$ and $\theta = 1$, $\pi = 5$ when $\mu = \infty$ (the NE and LQG solutions), while $\tau = 10$ when $\mu = \lambda$ (the H^∞ solution).

are legion. Thus, the policymaker avoids Nash inflation by inducing frequent escapes, but at the cost of periods of even higher inflation and considerable volatility. The solution clearly shows that in comparison to Figure 1, (approximately) H^∞ control—the most extreme conception of uncertainty aversion—is an excessive response to the model uncertainty that is generated by the monetary authority's not understanding his or her own role in the data generating process. Figure 3b, however, is more similar to Figure 1. For example, over the 4,000 periods shown, Figure 3b shows seven escapes from the Nash equilibrium. The Ramsey inflation rate remains at zero implying that robust control of unstructured model uncertainty results in larger swings in inflation than under LQG control, even when the preference for robustness is relatively mild. As we should expect from equation (29), the inflation rate at the Nash equilibrium is higher than in the LQG case, but lower than in the H^∞ case, because it varies positively with the policy maker's preference for robustness. A lower value of μ also tends to accelerate the dynamics of escapes for precisely the same reason: As suggested by Williams (2003), a higher preference for robustness leads to a more reactive response of inflation to revisions in γ, speeding the progress toward the Nash equilibrium level, and increasing the frequency of escapes.

We shall have something to say about the welfare implications of this policy response a bit later, but the suggestion here is that robust policy in the sense of Hansen and Sargent (2002) is not the right medicine for the comparatively mild specification error that is being committed here. Whether this negative outcome to this approach to model uncertainty is germane to this problem or applies to a broader set of conceivable model misspecifications would appear to be a useful line of research.[19]

---

19. Our finding may explain why quantitative applications of robust control of this type have focussed on events that lie outside of American monetary experience, namely various hyperinflations and financial crises. See, e.g., Kasa (2003) and Marcet and Nicolini (2003).

Figure 3a
Robust Response to Unstructured Model Uncertainty
(Robustness preference, $\mu = \lambda + 0.01$)

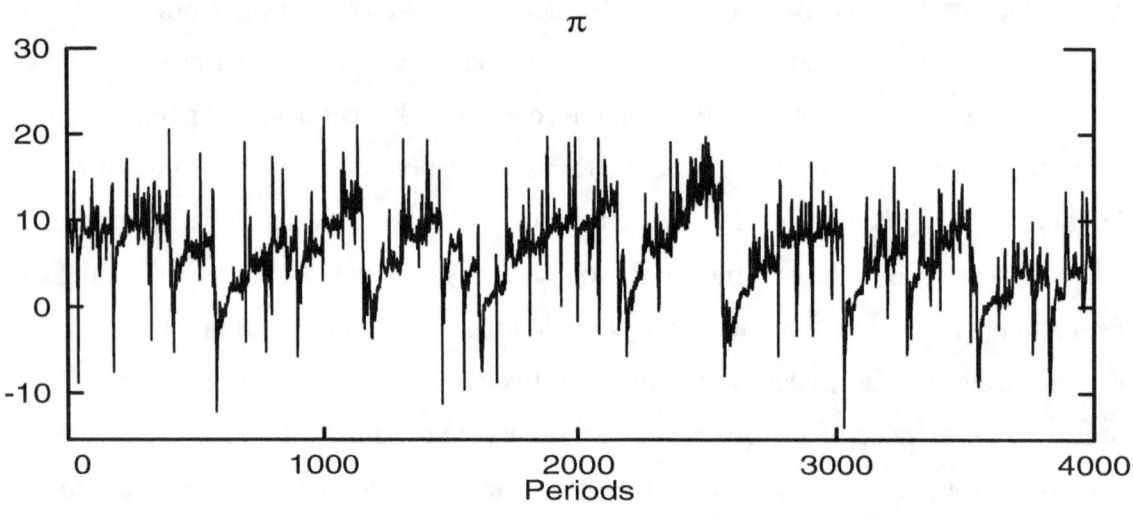

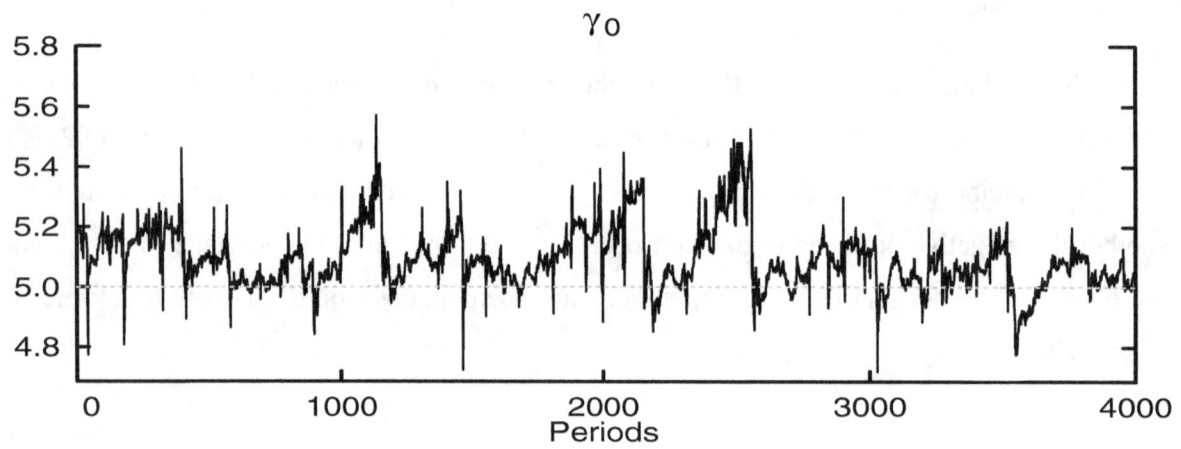

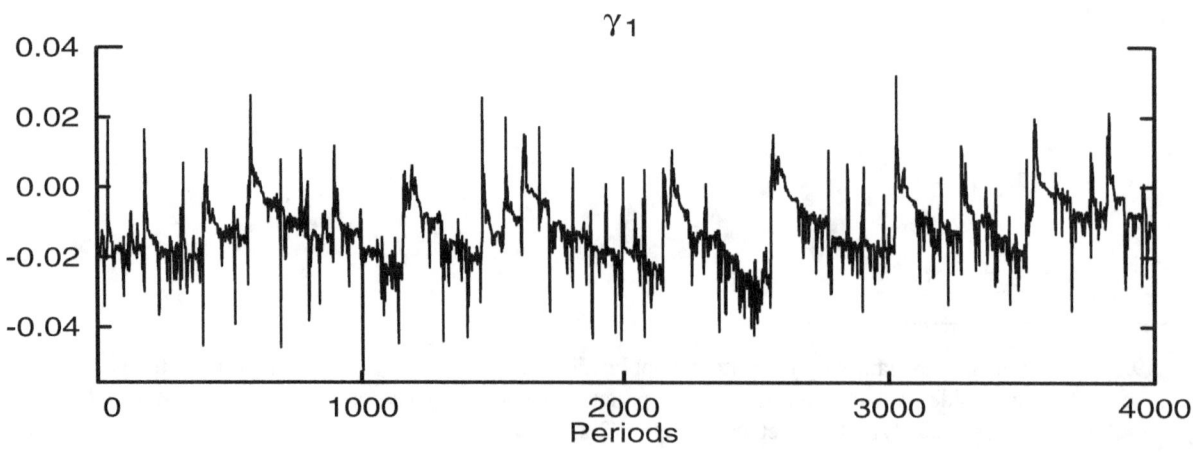

Figure 3b
Robust Response to Unstructured Model Uncertainty
(Robustness preference, $\mu = \lambda + 0.1$)

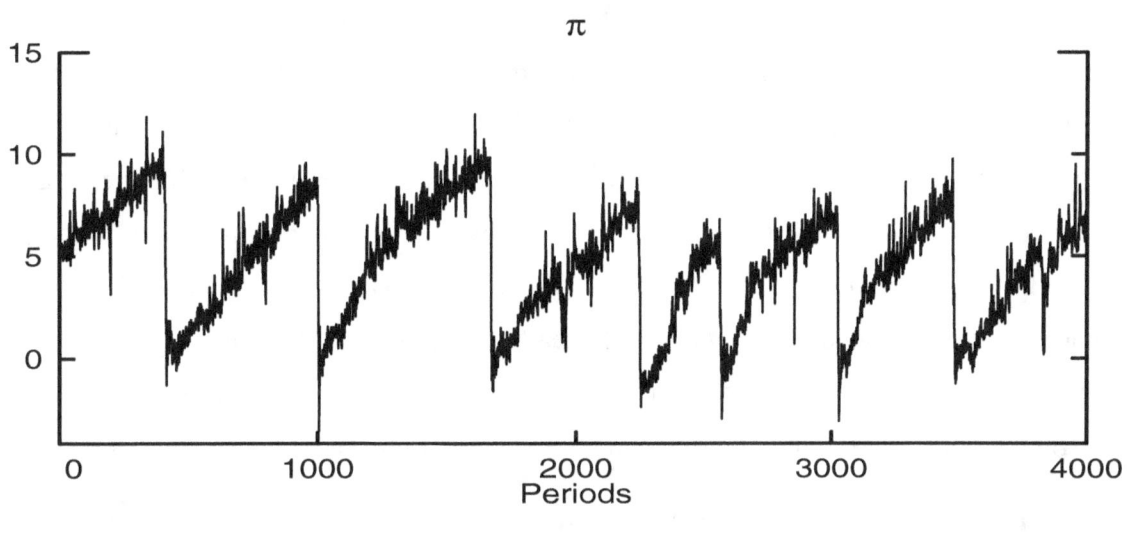

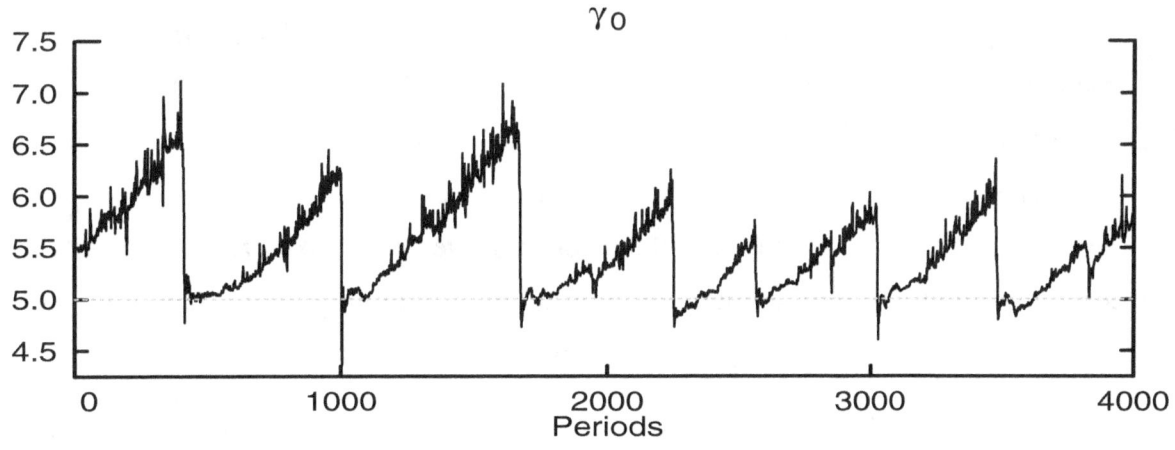

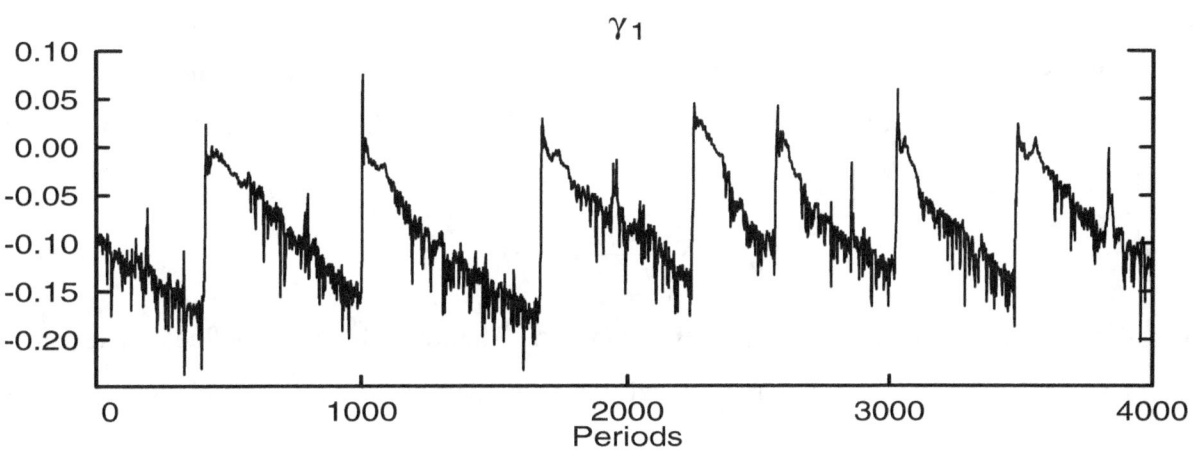

3. Controlling an Uncertain Economy

3.6 robust policy II: structured model uncertainty

In the previous subsection, the authority was assumed to have no knowledge of the location of Knightian uncertainty. Here we relax this restriction by allowing the authority to conjecture that the form of its model is correct, but the coefficients may be wrong. In this regard, our policymaker facing *structured model uncertainty* shares some characteristics with the Bayesian authority. In particular, both policymakers narrow the focus of their attention to the two coefficients, the γ, We might add that in so doing, the authority's assumption regarding the location of the uncertainty is aligned with what is being updated over time by the estimation procedure. But unlike the Bayesian controller, here the authority is assumed to be unable (or unwilling) to assign a probability distribution over parameters. Instead, we shall assume that a range of possible parameters is posited. The policymaker in this sub-section utilizes a robust policy rule that is less parametric than the Bayesian but more than the unstructured robust controller.

There are several variations on structured model uncertainty that one could adopt. Some, like Onatski (1999), Onatski and Stock (2000), and Tetlow and von zur Muehlen (2001) use a stability maximization criterion whereby the policymaker chooses the feedback parameters to maximize the range of models for which the economy is stable. Others, like von zur Muehlen (1982), Giannoni (2000, 2002), Svensson (2001) and Tetlow and von zur Muehlen (2001) assume a performance maximization criterion, where a standard loss function is minimized but conditioned on, once again, a malevolent nature choosing the set of parameters that maximizes the authority's loss function. Our formulation shares some characteristics with all of the papers named in the preceding sentence, but the closest counterpart for what we do is Giannoni (2002).

As in Giannoni (2001, 2002), we assume that the authority chooses as its upper and lower parameter bounds the mean value of the estimates of γ, plus and minus a scalar, δ, times the estimated standard error of coefficients, $\text{diag}(\sigma)$. Note, however, that unlike in the existing literature, the estimates of the coefficients, the standard errors, and the upper and lower bounds, all vary over time and are conditioned on the constant-gain learning. Formally, the upper bound for a parameter γ_i is:

$$\bar{\gamma}_{it} \in \sum_{t=0}^{\tau} \frac{\gamma_{it}}{\tau+1} + \delta \cdot \sigma_{i,t} \tag{32}$$

where σ_i is the *i*th diagonal element of the matrix σ. The lower bound is defined analogously. Giannoni (2002) shows, for a different model than this one, that nature's best choice (the worst case for the authority) will always be one of the corner solutions within the range of possible parameter values, a finding that we confirmed for our model. So nature, in her malevolence, chooses $\gamma_i, i = 1, 2$ among the combinations $\{\underline{\gamma}_0, \underline{\gamma}_1\}$, $\{\underline{\gamma}_0, \bar{\gamma}_1\}$, $\{\bar{\gamma}_0, \underline{\gamma}_1\}$ and $\{\bar{\gamma}_0, \bar{\gamma}_1\}$, to *maximize* the loss function:

$$L_t = E\left[\frac{1}{2}\lambda(\gamma_0 + \gamma_1 \pi)^2 + \pi^2\right] \tag{33}$$

given the monetary authority's best response, π^s, where the *s* superscript designates the solution for the *s*tructured-uncertainty problem. It turns out that for any choice of π^s, the loss-maximizing set of the boundary parameters, γ^s is the upper bound for both parameters when the last observed inflation rate is positive, $\pi_{t-1} > 0$, and the upper bound for γ_0 and the lower bound for γ_1, when $\pi_{t-1} < 0$. Formally, this means that all dates *t*:

$$\{\gamma_0^s, \gamma_1^s\} = \sup_{\langle \gamma_i \rangle} L = \left\{\bar{\gamma}_0, \begin{matrix} \bar{\gamma}_1 \text{ iff } (\pi_{t-1} \geq 0) \\ \underline{\gamma}_1 \text{ iff } (\pi_{t-1} < 0) \end{matrix}\right\} \tag{34}$$

Given this combination of worst-case parameters, the best response by the monetary authority is a feedback rule of the same form as equation (19), but with the parameterization governed by the boundary values specified by equation (34):

$$\hat{\pi}_t^s = \begin{cases} -\lambda \bar{\gamma}_0 \bar{\gamma}_1 / (1 + \lambda \bar{\gamma}_1^2) & \text{for } (\pi_{t-1} \geq 0) \\ -\lambda \bar{\gamma}_0 \underline{\gamma}_1 / (1 + \lambda \underline{\gamma}_1^2) & \text{for } (\pi_{t-1} < 0) \end{cases} \tag{35}$$

Figure 4a shows the implications of this robust response to structured model uncertainty for the traditional boundary width $\delta = 2$. The sign switching of the worst-case value of γ_1 against which the policymaker protects itself produces a similar switching in the inflation rate, so that inflation is very volatile. At the same time, however, the average inflation rate is zero, meaning that the robust policy maker is able to avoid Nash inflation, albeit at the cost of substantial volatility.

Before leaving this subject and turning to the welfare implications of these policies, it is useful to consider the implications of an alternative choice for δ, the width of the standard error band from which the authority picks best and worst case policies. Figure 4b shows the results for a much narrower band width, $\delta = 0.2$. In this instance, the monetary authority is unable to prevent a creep upward toward the Nash inflation rate.

Figure 4a
Robust Response to Structured Model Uncertainty
($\delta = 2$)

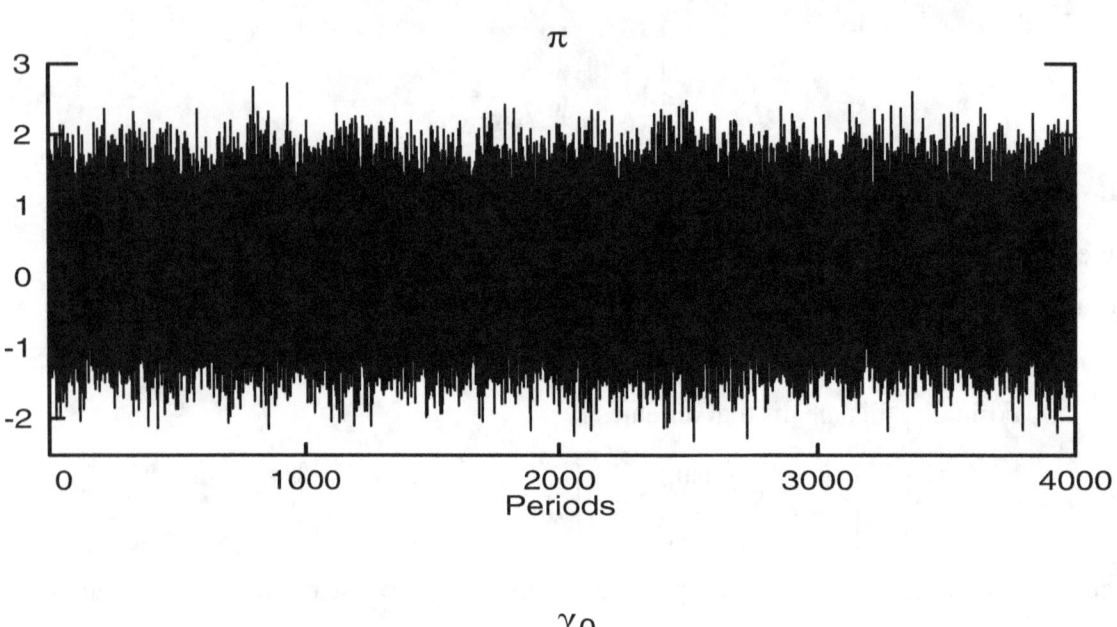

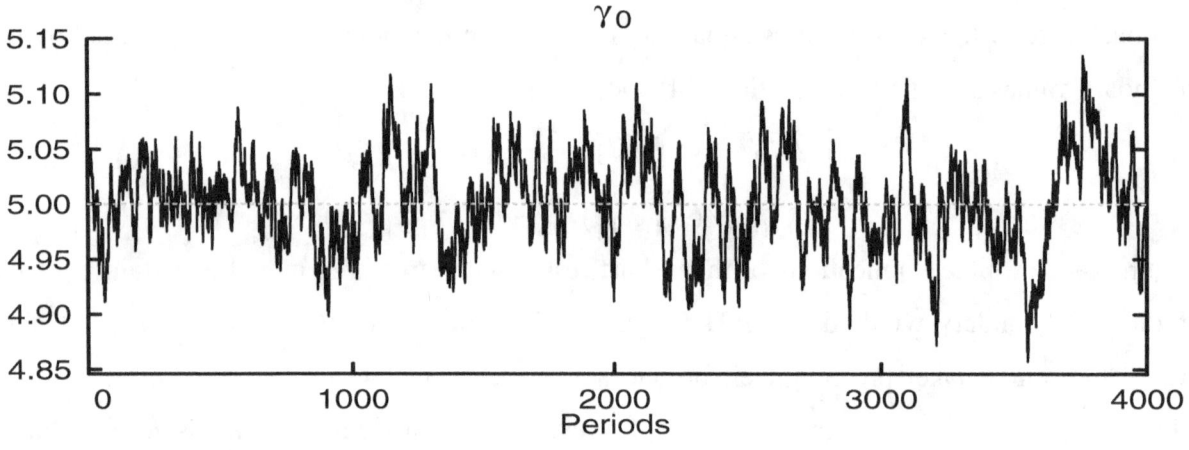

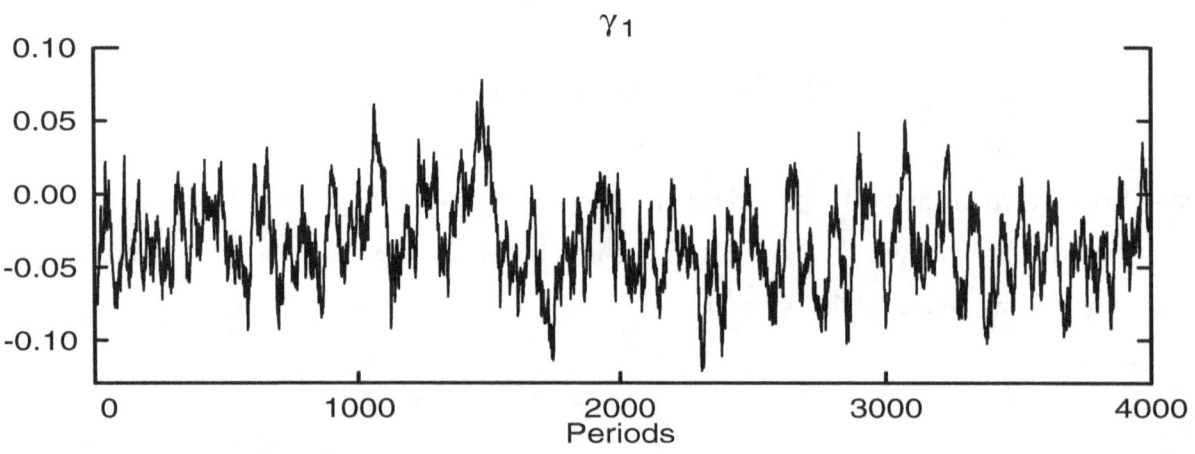

3. Controlling an Uncertain Economy

Figure 4b
Robust Response to Structured Model Uncertainty
($\delta = 0.2$)

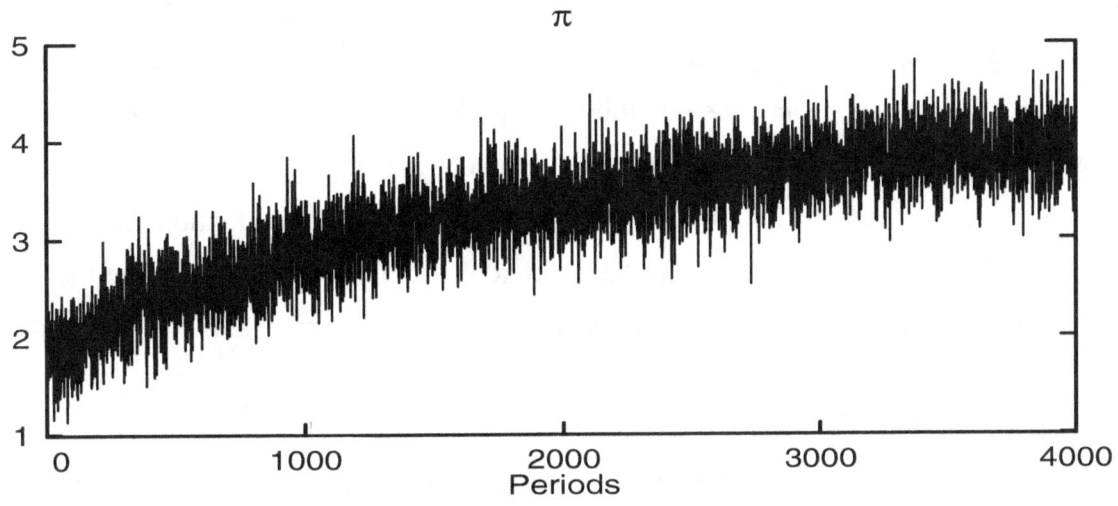

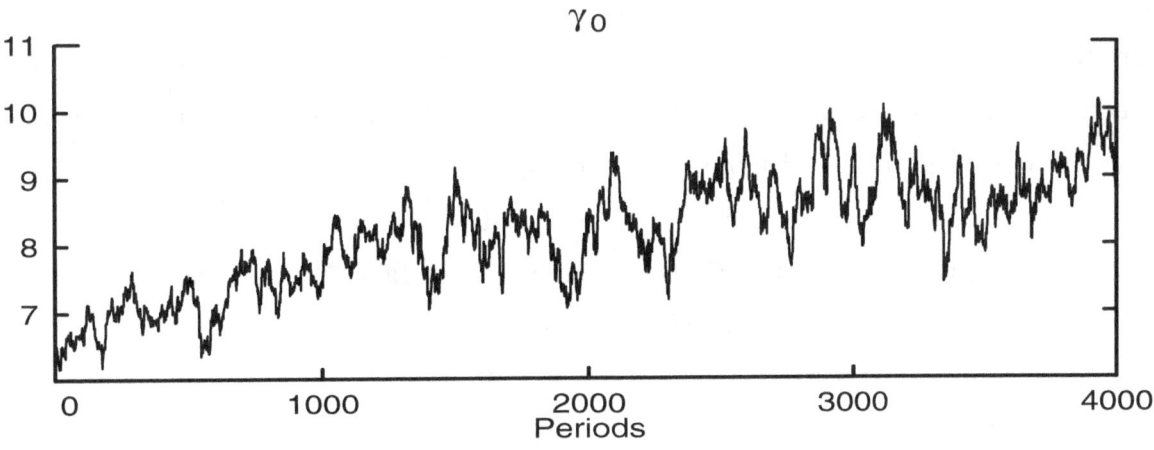

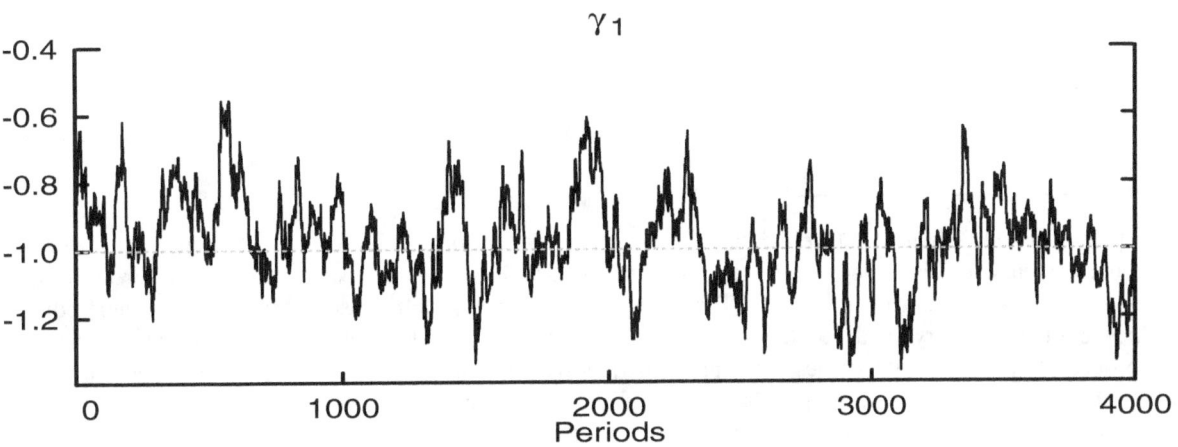

The logic of the result is straightforward: when δ is large enough, the authority acts as though inflation could be near the Nash rate and decides, therefore, not to produce the sequence of inflation surprises to bring the inflation rate up to the Nash equilibrium. And while this policy induces a great deal of volatility in inflation, the resulting imprecision in the estimated slope parameter helps ensure that policy remains protective against high inflation. When δ is small, the authority does not protect against the possibility of the Nash inflation, or something like it. This induces the same sequence of inflation surprises as under the certainty-equivalent policy, albeit somewhat smaller so that inflation creeps up slowly. The poor control of inflation, however, is not accompanied by a substantial increase in the standard error of the estimated γ_1, so that having gotten "behind the curve" on inflation in the early going, there is no mechanism to catch up.[20]

3.7 welfare: a summing up

The figures do a reasonable job of summarizing the performance of the economy. Most of what one needs to know to assess policy can be gleaned from the extremities of inflation that are reached in the simulations and the incidence of disinflations. Nevertheless, it is interesting to examine the extent to which welfare is affected, *ex post*, by the use of tools for handling model uncertainties. To this end, we computed the losses from the stochastic simulations shown in the figures using the *ex post* calculation of equation (3), averaged over time. As in the figures, five thousand observations were computed with the first 1000 discarded; the same set of stochastic shocks was used for each exercise. The results are shown in Table 1 below where the answer for the LQG rule has been normalized to unity without loss of generality.

---

20. Sargent and Williams (2003) find that through altering the prior distribution for γ by replacing the discounted recursive least squares equations, (11) and (12), with Kalman filters, the pattern and direction of escapes can be dramatically influenced. They concern themselves with the case of certainty-equivalent policies, but the boundary widths on the parameters chosen by the structured robust policy maker here can be loosely interpreted along the lines of the prior distributions in their paper. As in our case, the occurrence of escapes and the sustainability of the self-fulfilling equilibrium in their paper depend on the prior for the slope parameter (here, the supports of the slope parameter).

Table 1
Comparative loss from alternative approaches to model uncertainty

	Experiment	Parameter settings	H^2 loss
(1)	Certainty equivalent (LQG)	$\mu = \infty$	1
(2)	Bayesian	$\mu = \infty; \psi = 1$	1.07
(3)	Bayesian	$\mu = \infty; \psi = 5$	1.26
(4)	Unstructured robust	$\mu = \lambda + 0.1$	1.64
(5)	Unstructured robust	$\mu = \lambda + 0.01$	2.52
(6)	Structured robust	$\delta = 2$	0.90
(7)	Structured robust	$\delta = 0.2$	1.10
	memo items:		
(8)	Ramsey equilibrium	n/a	0.77
(9)	Nash equilibrium	n/a	1.54

Notes: These are the results from stochastic simulations of the model for 5000 dates and discarding the first 1000 observations, evaluating equation (3).

To begin, let us compare our base-case LQG policy against the hypothetical results where private agents believe in the Nash equilibrium or the Ramsey equilibrium. Comparing the two memo items at the bottom of the table shows the gains that would accrue to the monetary authority if it were able to commit to the Ramsey equilibrium. Whether measured against the Nash equilibrium result, or the certainty equivalent (or LQG) result, the benefits of commitment, if it were feasible, are substantial.

The rest of the table shows that all of the approaches that take uncertainty seriously nonetheless bring about no improvement in policy performance with the exception of one of the structured robust control results, shown in line (6).[21] The unstructured robust control approaches to the induction problem are uniformly deleterious, with results that might be described as very poor when the authority is particularly uncertainty averse. That said, even the case in line (5) where $\mu = \lambda + 0.1$ is one of fairly substantial uncertainty aversion; its loss, while consequential, is far from catastrophic. This suggests that the small doses of unstructured robust policymaking to hedge against misspecifications *other than the one studied here* would not come at great cost.

Table 2 below allows us to study the relationship between the preference for robustness under the uncertainty aversion of a Bayesian policy maker on the one hand and unstructured robust control policy maker on the other. Uncertainty aversion of the Bayesian variety is indexed by $\psi > 1$ with higher values representing greater degrees of aversion, and is summarized in the left-hand panel of the table. Increasing uncertainty aversion in Knightian sense is characterized by the choice of $\mu > \lambda$ with low values of μ being associated with higher degrees of uncertainty aversion; results for these policies are shown on the right-hand side of the table. The first row of the table shows that the certainty equivalence results are nested in both policies. As we move down the table, however, we see that both policies feature increasing deterioration in policy performance as the degree of uncertainty aversion increases. The second and fifth columns of the table show the number of escapes under each policy, given the preference for robustness. The Bayesian policy features fewer and fewer escapes as ψ rises. The unstructured robust authority, on the other hand, experiences more and more escapes as its preference for robustness increases. Yet in both cases, overall performance deteriorates with increasing uncertainty aversion. In short, neither policy is capable of overcoming the Nash inflation problem.

---

21. Qualitatively speaking, none of these results depend on the length of the simulation. However, the extent to which the structured robust control with $\delta = 0.2$ underperforms relative to the LQG policy climbs with the length of the simulation because the inflation rate asymptotes to the Nash inflation rate.

Table 2
Performance of Bayesian and Unstructured Robust Policies as a Function of Risk or Uncertainty Aversion

Bayesian Control			Unstructured Robust Control		
(1)	(2)	(3)	(4)	(5)	(6)
ψ	escape	loss	μ	escape	loss
0	5	1	∞	5	1
1	4	1.07	6	5	1.03
2	3	1.14	2	5	1.22
5	1	1.26	1.5	5	1.40
10	0	1.53	1.1	7	1.64
20	0	1.61	1.05	9	1.86
50	0	1.70	1.01	many	2.53

Notes: ψ is the multiple by which the standard error of the estimated coefficients in multiplied by as a hedge against misspecification prior to choosing the policy rule under Bayesian control; μ is the preference for robustness parameter under unstructured robust control, with $\mu = \infty$ corresponding with no preference for robustness at all (the linear-quadratic Gaussian policy) and $\mu \to \lambda$ corresponding to the most uncertainty averse (H^∞) solution.

Table 3
Performance of Structured Robust Policies as a function of Boundary Width

δ	Normalized loss
0	1.22
.1	1.23
.2	1.10
.25	.79
.5	.81
1	.84
2	.90
3	.97

Notes: mapping of boundary width, δ, where δ is the multiple of the standard error of estimated parameter, γ_1, against loss normalized such that under linear-quadratic-Gaussian control is equal to unity.

Table 3 demonstrates the influence of δ on performance under structured robust control. Recall that δ is the multiple of estimated standard errors around the sample means of the γ_i that the authority sets as the boundaries within which the true model parameters may lie. The table reveals a backward-bending relationship between δ and the normalized loss. The reasons are as noted in the previous subsection: when δ is "too low", there is insufficient protection against Nash-like inflation to prevent a drift upward in inflation and once this drift is ongoing, the precision in the estimated γ_i is quite low. Deteriorating economic performance does not induce increasing uncertainty aversion because the worsening conditions do not manifest themselves in less precise coefficient estimates. Once the value of δ reaches a certain threshold, protection against Nash inflation is established and the average inflation rate is zero. For this model and its calibration, it takes relatively little uncertainty aversion (defined as it is here) to prevent an upward creep in inflation. Once this minimal level of δ is established, any further increases are uniformly deleterious to performance.

More generally, the results show that the appropriate response of monetary policy to uncertainty in a real-time environment like the one described by Chairman Greenspan in the quotation that opened this article requires some knowledge of the origins of the misspecification against which the authority seeks protection. The Bayesian policy response to model uncertainty does not improve policy because the problem the policymaker is trying to solve is not one of sampling error; the fluctuations in the estimated parameters are not random in the way the Bayesian assumes. This much is not surprising, at least after the fact. What is perhaps a bit more surprising is that it is not the case that designing policy to protect misspecification of completely unknown origins will lead to improvements in performance relative to ignoring the misspecification in the first place. Rather, we have found that the policy maker needs to come to terms with the sources of misspecification in broad terms in order to ensure an improvement in policy performance.

4. Concluding remarks

This paper has examined robust policy design in the presence of misspecification and learning in a quasi-real-time environment. Our testing ground has been a re-examination of Thomas Sargent's explanation of the great inflation of the 1970s and its "conquest" in the 1980s. In the original work, the monetary authority was assumed to re-estimate his or her reference model in such a way as to suggest doubts about the constancy of the estimated parameters. And yet the policymaker was not allowed to carry forward those doubts to the question of policy design. We have relaxed this restriction by allowing the monetary authority to seek protection against model misspecification in three possible ways.

First, the policymaker was permitted to take the estimated standard errors of the parameters into account when designing policy, as a Bayesian would do. In this regard, we investigated the advice of Blinder (1998), based on Brainard (1967), among others. We found that contrary to conventional wisdom, responding to model uncertainty via the Bayesian approach produced results that differ only in small ways from the certainty equivalent case. This result obtains despite a modeling structure, with discounted history, that biases upward, in some sense, the standard errors that condition the Bayesian response, and despite the fact that the Bayesian policy maker has correctly assumed the location of the misspecification. We conclude that if policy makers, operating in a world of uncertainty, were to follow Blinder's advice to "do less" than the certainty equivalent policy response to shocks, and did so using the usual Bayesian statistical criteria, they would find no relief from their problem. The reason the Bayesian response to model uncertainty is not successful is straightforward: it is designed to counter misspecification in the form of random coefficients when the problem here, rather than being random in this sense, is induced by the authority's failure to recognize its role as a part of the data generating process. Moreover, our checks of robustness of this result, combined with some hints in the literature, suggest that this finding is likely to have pertinence beyond the current setting.

Second, we allowed the policy maker to entertain uncertainty in the sense of Knight, using two different formulations. In one formulation, we allowed the policy maker to use unstructured robust control, meaning that we allowed him or her to protect against modeling errors of uncertain magnitude and unknown origin. In this instance, we were following a line of research by Hansen and Sargent (1995, 2002) on handling model uncertainty. In the other formulation, we allowed the policymaker to protect against structured modeling errors, meaning the errors were in a known location, but with no prior knowledge regarding the magnitude of the misspecification. In this instance, we were following a line of research by von zur Muehlen (1982) and Giannoni (2001, 2002).

We found that protecting against model misspecification of the Hansen-Sargent variety resulted in a deterioration of economic performance in all senses of the term. The robust response to uncertainty of unspecified origin resulted in higher average levels of inflation, more frequent escapes and thus more volatility. Economic performance as measured by evaluating the authority's loss function was worse than performance under the certainty-equivalent policy. This finding suggests that the kind of misspecification entertained in Sargent (1999), Cho, Williams and Sargent (2002) and adopted here is not severe enough to justify the Hansen-Sargent (1995, 2002) treatment: the medicine of robust policy is worse than the disease.[22] On the surface of it, this is a surprising result since it is arguably this sort of specification error that this approach was meant to handle. Recently, however, there have been indications that the kind of hands-off, completely non-parametric approach has its drawbacks. Onatski and Williams (2003) and Levin and Williams (2003) suggest that unstructured robust control needs to be used with care.

The results for structured robust control, that is robust policy making as envisioned by Giannoni (2002) among others, are intriguing. There, we found that a small, judiciously chosen degree of preference for robustness can result in the avoidance of Nash inflation and an improve-

---

22. That performance under uncertainty-sensitive policy design with a misspecified model could still be worse than if the possibility of misspecification were ignored was certainly not an implausible outcome; Kilponen (2001), for example, notes this can arise.

4. Concluding remarks

ment in overall economic performance. At the same time, a high degree of inflation variability must be tolerated. These results suggest that a policy maker that investigates the sources of misspecification can improve policy outcomes even if he or she cannot correct the specification error directly, provided that some narrowing down of the sources of the misspecification is possible.

Taken together the results here strengthen the Sargent explanation for the inflation of the 1970s. Had the recurring bouts of Nash inflation followed by bouts of disinflation disappeared with the economy under the control of many or all of these policies, the results would have suggested that Sargent's findings were a manifestation of the assumed naiveté of the policy maker. And while it is reasonable to question whether central bankers would forget the lessons of history and allow high inflation to re-assert itself, it is worth noting that commentary describing inflation as yesterday's war abounds. Furthermore, well-known economists such as Ray Fair (1999) and William Brainard and George Perry (2000), all known to offer policy advice on macroeconomic issues, question the validity of the natural rate hypothesis, very much along the lines predicted by Sargent.

5. References:

Adam, Klaus (2002) "On the Relationship Between Robust and Bayesian Decision Making" Center for Financial Studies working paper no. 2003-02, Goethe University, Frankfurt am Maim, Germany (December 2002).

Barro, Robert J. and David B. Gordon (1983) "A positive theory of inflation in a natural rate model" 91,*Journal of Political Economy*,4 (August), pp. 589-610.

Beck, Guenter W. and Wolker Wieland (2002) "Learning, Stabilization and Credibility: Optimal Monetary Policy in a Changing Economy" unpublished manuscript, Goethe University of Frankfurt.

Blinder, Alan (1987) *Hard Heads, Soft Hearts: tough-minded economics for a just society* (Reading, MA: Addison-Wesley).

Blinder, Alan (1998) *Central Banking in Theory and Practice* (Cambridge, MA: MIT Press).

Brainard, William (1967) "Uncertainty and the Effectiveness of Monetary Policy" 57,*American Economic Review*,2 (May), pp. 411-425.

Brainard, William and George Perry (2000) "Making Policy in a Changing World" in G. Perry and J. Tobin (eds.) *Economic Events, Ideas and Policies: the 1960s and after* (Washington: Brookings Institution Press).

Bullard, James and In-Koo Cho (2001) "Escapist Policy Rules" unpublished manuscript, Federal Reserve Bank of St. Louis (December).

Caravani, P. (1995) "On H-infinity criteria for macroeconomic policy evaluation" 19,*Journal of Economic Dynamics and Control*,5/7 (July/September), pp. 961-984.

Christiano, Lawrence and Christopher Gust (2000) "The Expectations Trap Hypothesis" 25,*Federal Reserve Bank of Chicago Economic Perspectives*,2 (2nd quarter), pp. 21-39.

Cho, In-Koo; Noah Williams, and Thomas J. Sargent (2002) "Escaping Nash Inflation" 70,*Review of Economic Studies*,2 (April), p. 1-40.

Chow, Gregory C. (1973) "Effect of Uncertainty on Optimal Control Policies" 14,*International Economic Review*,3 (October), pp. 632-645.

Cogley, Timothy and Thomas J. Sargent (2001) "Evolving Post-World War II U.S. Inflation Dynamics" in B. S. Bernanke and K. Rogoff (eds.) *NBER Macroeconomics Annual 2001* pp. 331-373.

Craine, Roger (1977) "Optimal Monetary Policy with Uncertainty" 1,*Journal of Economic Dynamics and Control*,1 (February), pp. 59-83.

De Long, J. Bradford (1997) "America's peace-time inflation: the 1970s" in Christina D. Romer and David H. Romer (eds.) *Reducing Inflation: motivation and strategy* NBER Studies in Business Cycles, volume 30 (Chicago: University of Chicago Press), pp. 247-276.

Drew, Aaron and Benjamin Hunt (1999) "Efficient Simple Monetary Policy Rules and the Implications of Potential Output Uncertainty" Reserve Bank of New Zealand working paper no. G99/5 (August).

Fair, Ray C. (1999) "Testing the NAIRU Model for the United States" 82,*Review of Economics and Statistics*,1 (February), pp. 64-71.

Gerali, Andrea and Francesco Lippi (2001) "On the 'Conquest' of Inflation" CEPR working paper no. 3101 (December).

Giannoni, Marc P. (2001) "Robust Optimal Monetary Policy in a Forward-looking Model with Parameter and Shock Uncertainty" unpublished manuscript, Stern School of Business, New York University.

Giannoni, Marc P. (2002) "Does model uncertainty justify caution?: robust optimal policy in a forward-looking model" 6,*Macroeconomic Dynamics*,1 (February).

Gilboa, I. and D. Schmeidler (1989) "Maxmin Expected Utility with a Nonunique Prior" 18,*Journal of Mathematical Economics*,2 pp. 141-153.

Greenspan, Alan (2001) "Monetary Policy in the Face of Uncertainty" 21,*Cato Journal*,2 (Fall), pp. 161-168.

Hall, Simon; Christopher Salmon; Tony Yates and Nicoletta Batini (1999) "Uncertainty and Simple Monetary Policy Rules: an illustration for the United Kingdom" Bank of England working paper no. 96 (June).

Hansen, Lars Peter and Thomas J. Sargent (1995) "Discounted linear exponential quadratic gaussian control" 40,*IEEE Transactions on Automatic Control*, pp. 968-971.

Hansen, Lars Peter and Thomas J. Sargent (2002) *Robust Control and Model Uncertainty in Macroeconomics* unpublished manuscript, October.

Hansen, Lars Peter; Thomas J. Sargent, and T. Tallarini (1999) "Robust Permanent Income and Pricing" 66,*Review of Economic Studies*, pp. 873-907.

Hansen, Lars Peter; Thomas J. Sargent, and N. E. Wang (2002) "Robust Permanent Income and Pricing with Filtering" 6,*Macroeconomic Dynamics*,1 (February).

Ireland, Peter (1999) "Does the time-consistency problem explain the behavior of inflation in the United States?" 44,*Journal of Monetary Economics*,2 (October), pp. 279-292.

Kasa, Kenneth (2003) "Learning, Large Deviations and Recurrent Currency Crises" unpublished manuscript, forthcoming in *International Economic Review.*

Kilponen, Juha (2001) "A Positive Theory of a Risk Sensitive Central Banker" unpublished manuscript, City University Business School, London, U.K.

Kydland, Finn E. and Edward Prescott (1977) "Rules Rather than Discretion: the inconsistency of optimal plans" 85,*Journal of Political Economy* pp. 473-493.

Levin, Andrew; Volker Wieland and John C. Williams (1999) "Robustness of Simple Monetary Policy Rules under Model Uncertainty" in J.B. Taylor (ed.) Monetary Policy Rules (Chicago: University of Chicago Press), pp. 263-299.

Levin, Andrew; Volker Wieland and John C. Williams (2001) "The Performance of Forecast-based Monetary Policy Rules under Model Uncertainty" European Central Bank working paper no. 68, forthcoming in *American Economic Review.*

Levin, Andrew and John C. Williams (2003) "On the Robustness of Robust Control" unpublished manuscript, Federal Reserve Bank of San Francisco.

Lucas, Robert E. (1972) "Econometric Testing of the Natural Rate Hypothesis" in Otto Eckstein (ed.) *Econometrics of Price Determination* (Washington: Board of Governors of the Federal Reserve System), pp. 50-59.

Lucas, Robert E. (1976) "Econometric Policy Evaluation: a critique" 1,*Carnegie-Rochester Conference Series on Public Policy.* pp. 19-46.

Marcet, Albert and Juan Pablo Nicolini (2003) "Recurrent Hyperinflations and Learning" unpublished manuscript dated 1998, forthcoming in *American Economic Review.*

Martin, Ben (1999) "Caution and Gradualism in Monetary Policy Under Uncertainty" Bank of England working paper no. 125 (December).

Onatski, Alexei (1999) "Minimax Analysis of Model Uncertainty: comparison to Bayesian approach, worst possible economies, and optimal robust monetary policies" unpublished manuscript, Department of Economics, Harvard University.

5. References:

Onatski, Alexei and James H. Stock (2002) "Robust Monetary Policy under Model Uncertainty in a Small Model of the U.S. Economy" 6,*Macroeconomic Dynamics*,1 (February)

Onatski, Alexei and Noah Williams (2003) "Modeling Model Uncertainty" NBER working paper no. 9566 (March).

Orphanides, Athanasios; David Reifschneider, Robert Tetlow, John C. Williams and Frederico Finan (2000) "Errors in the Measurement of the Output Gap and the Design of Monetary Policy" 52,*Journal of Economics and Business,*2 pp. 117-141.

Rudebusch, Glenn (2001) "Is the Fed Too Timid?: monetary policy in an uncertain world" 83,*Review of Economics and Statistics*,2 (May) pp. 203-217.

Sack, Brian (2000) "Does the Fed Act Gradually?: a VAR analysis" 46,*Journal of Monetary Economics*,1 pp. 229-256.

Sargent, Thomas J. (1971) "A Note on the 'Accelerationist Controversy'" 3,*Journal of Money, Credit and Banking* pp. 721-725.

Sargent, Thomas J. (1999) *The Conquest of American Inflation* (Princeton: Princeton U. Press).

Sargent, Thomas J. and Noah Williams (2003) "Impacts of Priors on Convergence and Escapes from Nash Inflation" unpublished manuscript, New York University and Princeton University.

Schellekens, Phillip (1999) "Caution and Conservatism in the Making of Monetary Policy" unpublished manuscript, European Central Bank.

Shuetrim, Geoffrey and Christopher Thompson (2000) "The Implications of Uncertainty for Monetary Policy" in Benjamin Hunt and Adrian Orr (eds.) *Monetary Policy Under Uncertainty* (Wellington, NZ: Reserve Bank of New Zealand), pp. 259-292.

Smets, Frank (2000) "Output Gap Uncertainty: does it matter for the Taylor rule?" in Benjamin Hunt and Adrian Orr (eds.) *Monetary Policy Under Uncertainty* (Wellington, NZ: Reserve Bank of New Zealand), pp. 10-29.

Söderström, Ulf (2002) "Monetary Policy with Uncertain Parameters" 104,*Scandanavian Journal of Economics*,1 (March), pp. 125-145.

Srour, Gabriel (1999) "Inflation Targeting Under Uncertainty" *Bank of Canada Technical Report no. 85* (Ottawa: Bank of Canada).

Stock, James H. (1999) "Comment" in John B. Taylor (ed.) *Monetary Policy Rules* (Chicago: University of Chicago Press), pp. 253-259.

Svensson, Lars E.O. (2000) "Robust Control Made Simple" unpublished manuscript, Department of Economics, Princeton University.

Sworder, Daniel (1965) "Minmax Control of Discrete Time Stochastic Systems" *SIAM Journal of Applied Mathematics, Series A*, (Control 2), pp. 433-449.

5. References:

Taylor, John B. (1997) "Comment on 'America's Only Peacetime Inflation: the 1970s'" in Christina D. Romer and David H. Romer (eds.) *Reducing Inflation: motivation and strategy* NBER Studies in Business Cycles, volume 30 (Chicago: University of Chicago Press).

Taylor, John B. (1998) "Monetary Policy Guidelines for Unemployment and Inflation Stability" in Robert M. Solow and John B. Taylor (eds.) *Inflation, Unemployment and Monetary Policy* (Cambridge, MA: MIT Press)

Tetlow, Robert J. (2003) "Uncertain Potential Output and Monetary Policy in a Forward-looking Model" unpublished manuscript in revision, Division of Research and Statistics, Board of Governors of the Federal Reserve System.

Tetlow, Robert J. and Peter von zur Muehlen (2001a) "Simplicity Versus Optimality: the choice monetary policy rules when agents must learn" 25,*Journal of Economic Dynamics and Control*,1/2 pp. 245-279.

Tetlow, Robert J. and Peter von zur Muehlen (2001b) "Robust Monetary Policy with Misspecified Models: Does model uncertainty always call for attenuated policy? 25,*Journal of Economic Dynamics and Control*,6/7 pp. 911-949.

Tetlow, Robert J. and Peter von zur Muehlen (2003) "Bounded Rationality, Robust Policy Design and the Conquest of American Inflation" manuscript in preparation.

von zur Muehlen, Peter (1982) "Activist versus Nonactivist Monetary Policy: optimal rules under extreme uncertainty" manuscript now available as Finance and Economics Discussion Series paper no. 2001-02 (January).

Whittle, Peter (1990) *Risk-sensitive Optimal Control* (New York: Wiley).

Wieland, Volker (2003) "Monetary Policy and Uncertainty About the Natural Unemployment Rate" Center for Economic Policy Research discussion paper no. 3811.

Williams, Noah (2003) "Escape Dynamics in Learning Models" unpublished manuscript, Department of Economics, Princeton University.

5. References:

www.ingramcontent.com/pod-product-compliance
Lightning Source LLC
Chambersburg PA
CBHW081801170526
45167CB00008B/3279